6122

# THE·ART·OF
# LOUIS COMFORT
# TIFFANY

# THE·ART·OF
# LOUIS COMFORT
# TIFFANY

## VIVIENNE COULDREY

THE WELLFLEET PRESS

WELLFLEET

A QUANTUM BOOK

Published by Wellfleet Press
A Division of Book Sales Inc
114 Northfield Avenue
Edison, New Jersey 08837
USA

ISBN 1-55521-447-9

This book was produced by
Quantum Books Ltd
6 Blundell Street
London N7 9BH
Printed in China

"God has given us our talents, not to copy the talents of others, but rather to use our brains and our imagination in order to obtain the revelation of True Beauty."

LOUIS COMFORT TIFFANY

# CONTENTS

# FOREWORD

Louis Comfort Tiffany worked all his life to find a balance between his roles as artist and businessman. Tiffany became a world famous name but one that is very difficult to classify. He ran a business conforming to the wishes of customers, with large scale production organized to meet demands. Yet he was an artist of rare decorative gifts and technical skills and he created the famous Favrile blown glass of classic beauty.

He enjoyed the heights of popularity and critical acclaim at the turn of the century when no self-respecting household in America was complete without a Tiffany lamp or vase or window. He knew the depths of neglect and derision when his work ceased to be fashionable and many of his creations were destroyed.

He has left behind a legacy of technical brilliance and bold originality in the form of decorative art that is increasingly appreciated, and, therefore rising in value, today.

RIGHT: The Rose Bower Lamp — leaded glass shade of cabbage roses with sculptured bronze base, made in 1900. As well as being lovely to look at Tiffany lamps give a pleasing diffused quality to the light.

# FAMOUS FATHER, FAMOUS SON

"Reach boldly out and grasp the life about you."
GOETHE

Tiffany is a name that has become part of American legend. It is an attractive, evocative word, conveying something elegant, luxurious, turn-of-the-century stylish and desirable. The dictionary defines Tiffany, a word derived from Old French, as a kind of gauze or muslin, originally a fine dress worn on Twelfth Night and the manifestation of God at Epiphany.

It is an apt name for Tiffany the artist, who set out to create colour in glass, bring beauty into ordinary homes, and whose best work expressed emotion in abstract form.

Today the name Tiffany conveys several different things but there is a certain vagueness about the people behind the name. First, there is Tiffany the founder of the New York jewellery and silver store, the smartest place in the world to buy diamonds, which was immortalized by Truman Capote in his novel and Audrey Hepburn in the film *Breakfast at Tiffany's*, which has the same kind of status as tea at the Ritz, but is rather more racy.

Then there is Tiffany the artist, the foremost American exponent of Art Nouveau, creator of the beautiful Tiffany lamps and Favrile glass vases that achieve fantastically high prices in today's salerooms.

There was a famous father, Charles Lewis Tiffany, and a famous son, Louis Comfort Tiffany.

In 1837 Charles Lewis Tiffany founded the firm of Tiffany and Young, which was to become Tiffany & Co, the pre-eminent New York jewellers and silversmiths for the next century and a half. He became known as the King of Diamonds, catering for the crowned heads of Europe, buying their gems and jewellery when they lost their thrones, selling to the new American industrial barons and millionaire families — the Astors and the Vanderbilts — and advising presidents from the time of Abraham Lincoln.

Tiffany & Co was an expensive but not an exclusive and snobbish shop. It was essentially American and democratic. As well as displaying the million-dollar Tiffany Diamond in a velvet-lined case (not for sale), as well as providing for the extravagant tastes of the extravagantly wealthy American families, Charles Tiffany set out to cater for the popular market. And he was a shrewd entrepreneur. In the firm's early days he prowled round the New York docks, bargaining with sea captains and snapping up exotic imports from the

RIGHT: **The Zinnia Lamp — vibrantly colourful lamps like this one, with its inspiration of flowers, achieved Tiffany's aim of bringing beauty into the home.**

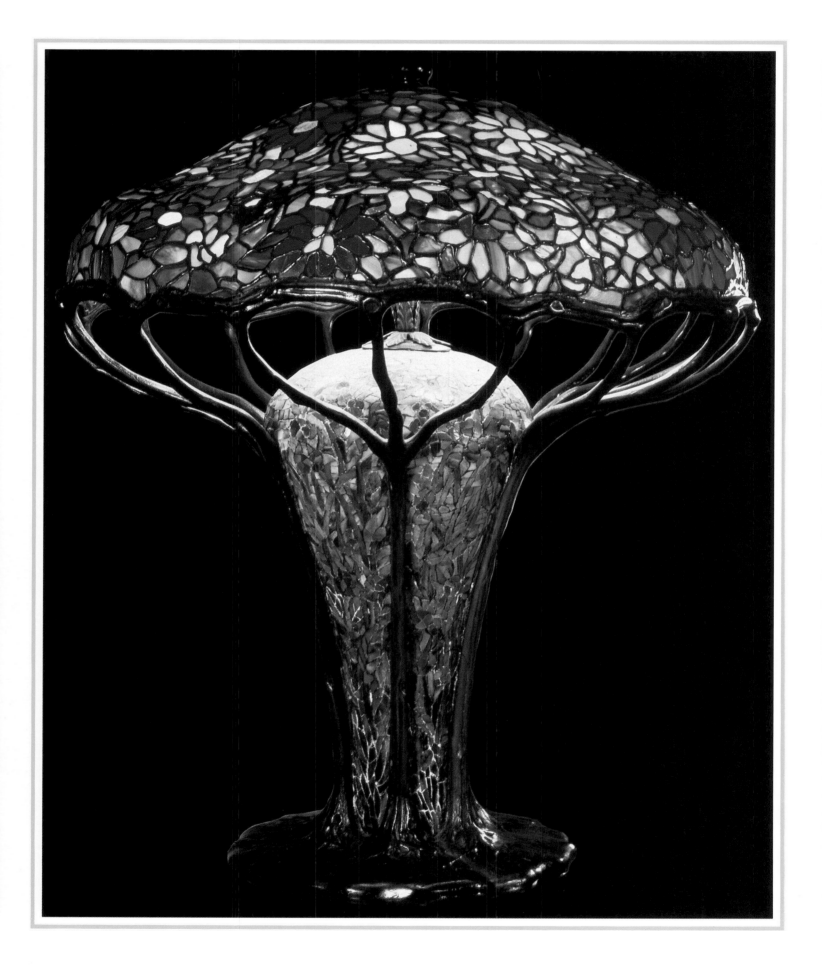

LEFT: Peacock Feather Vase — peacocks were a recurring theme in Art Nouveau and this vase is a remarkable achievement, giving the impression of pliable fronds of feathers in gleaming iridescent glass.

RIGHT: The beauty of this Favrile vase made in 1919 is in the subtle shimmering colours and the fluid abstract decoration.

LEFT: **Gold vases have a rich iridescent sheen and are silky to the touch.**

Orient — fans, carvings, Chinese umbrellas, novelties and curios. For the souvenir hunters he bought up the remains of the First Great Atlantic Cable in 1858, when the transatlantic telegraph link finally reached the Irish coast, and had them made into paperweights and bracelets. The police had to be called in to control the rush of customers.

Tiffany & Co had great influence on the development of silversmithing in the United States, promoting quality and design to match Europe and encouraging and commissioning American craftsmen. The firm made a fortune in the Civil War, supplying everything from cap badges to swords, and became the world's largest collector of precious stones.

Charles Tiffany acquired a well-deserved reputation for maintaining standards of quality, for foresight and integrity. He price-tagged even the most expensive jewellery. No haggling or discounts were allowed, even for presidents, as Dwight D. Eisenhower discovered; he was treated the same as every other customer.

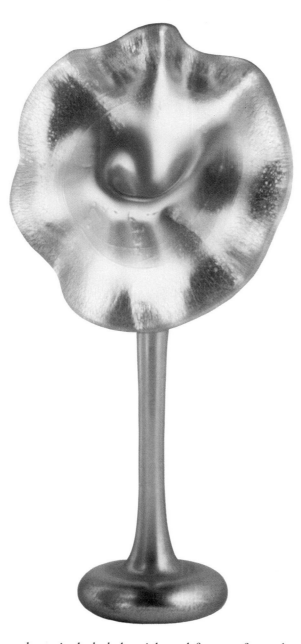

RIGHT: **Jack-in-the-pulpit vases were a very popular design. The spectacular petalled shape on a slender stem showed off Tiffany's iridescent glass in many different colour combinations.**

Customers have included the rich and famous from that time to this, among them, Jenny Lind, Ethel Merman, Elizabeth Taylor and John F. Kennedy. Tiffany's was the place where presidents selected the gifts to be given to foreign heads of state, because it was synonymous with quality and American craftsmanship. And in the days when diamonds were a girl's best friend, Tiffany's was the place to acquire them, because Tiffany's had class.

Louis Comfort Tiffany was born with a golden spoon in his mouth, as he said himself. He was brought up in an environment where beautiful things were appreciated, where arts and crafts and commerce mingled. He had a mind of his own, though, criticizing the work of the older generation, opposing the establishment and rejecting the commercial management role marked out for him by his father. He was determined that the life of an artist was the only one for him.

On leaving school in 1866 he began his art studies informally, taking up a brush and painting rather than following an academic course. He haunted

the studios of George Inness, listening to the talk among the younger artists of a new realism. Inness did not give instruction; he painted and talked at the same time, fired by a strong religious feeling, imparting his belief that the "true artistic impulse is divine".

Then Louis Tiffany set off on his travels, to Paris, Algiers and Venice, to Spain, Morocco, Palestine, Persia, Egypt and Italy. He travelled as a student of art but with all the advantages of wealth, security and his father's business connections, for Tiffany & Co had opened branches in Paris and London. His travels released the true artist in him, inspiring his future achievements and opening his eyes to the arts of antiquity.

He declared that his travels "gave a wrench to many prejudices imbibed from art school and academies in which the majority of men are blind followers". Louis Tiffany was certainly no blind follower.

He visited Europe at an exciting time, when many artists were deeply affected by Japanese influences and were under the spell of the Orient and Islam. He discovered for himself the exotic scenery of North Africa and the Moorish architecture of Spain.

At that time he would have seen the works of William Morris, Edward Burne-Jones, James McNeill Whistler and others who were breaking free from Victorian conventions and limitations, from the clutter of *objets d'art* copied from the classical, the Renaissance, the baroque and the rococo. Artists in the Arts and Crafts Movement were going back to nature with a fresh, new approach; in the Aesthetic Movement they were placing art and beauty above everything.

For Louis Tiffany all this was a powerful stimulus to the senses, arousing his creative force, and he set out to express it in the way that attracted him most — in glass and in colour.

He was amazed at the softly glowing, iridescent colours in Roman and Syrian glass, fascinated to discover how they had been achieved. He admired the rich colours of the mosaics of Byzantium and the glorious reds and blues of medieval stained-glass windows in gothic cathedrals, their brilliance and translucence. He also discovered how stained glass had become a dim, neglected art in northern Europe since the Renaissance and realized that here was a branch of art that might offer new fields of challenging work in the New

RIGHT: **Pond Lily Lamp with 12 lights of iridescent glass and sculptured lily-pad base. Tiffany's art brought a romantic beauty to the new invention of electric light at the turn-of-the-century.**

LEFT: The Apple Blossom Lamp. Multi-coloured glass makes the shade of blossoms, with bronze stem the trunk and spreading roots the base of the apple tree — the perfect unity of form.

ABOVE: The shade of the Magnolia Lamp which achieved a record auction price of $528,000 in 1985, confirming Tiffany as the most expensive form of Art Nouveau.

World, work that would give him the chance to develop his skill as a colourist. For Tiffany, colour was more important than form in art and for stained glass artists colour sense was the most vital. Colour in a window could be made radiant and dramatic when the light came through it.

His skill as a colourist emerged first in his paintings, but he was soon looking beyond the boundaries of fine art, turning to interior design. Among the wealthy families in the United States there was great scope for providing magnificent interiors and Louis Comfort Tiffany and his associates were soon in great demand, praised by the critics for harmonizing the various aspects of home decoration and for fresh, original ideas.

But all the time Tiffany was originating interior decor for the fashionable, he was also experimenting with glass. He found that the only way to obtain the kind of glass he wanted for stained-glass windows was to produce it himself, going back to 14th-century basics to learn how it was done. He built kilns and experimented with new formulas for pot-metal glass, the kind used for preserve jars and bottles, producing colour in varying degrees of translucency, making opalescent, semitransparent glass, and achieving, after many setbacks, Favrile glass. Many years of experimentation later, he found out how to avoid using paints, etching or burning, or otherwise treating the surface of the glass; the colour was in the glass itself, even the flesh tones for figures and faces.

There was enormous religious enthusiasm in America at this time and there were 4,000 churches under construction, all embellished with memorial windows. The enthusiasm for Tiffany stained-glass windows swept the country, particularly in churches with Biblical subjects but also in homes, schools, libraries and institutions. His windows won awards and praise on all sides. Boldly, Tiffany compared American glass with medieval glass: "I maintain the best American coloured windows are superior to the best medieval windows."

Tiffany was famous 100 years ago for his stained glass, and his first artistic love was his windows, but his fame today endures because of his small glass — Favrile vases and Tiffany lamps. Where there is universal critical acclaim for his Favrile glass, with its infinite variations of colour and richness, there is less enthusiasm now for the window designs in which it was used. Sometimes his

RIGHT: **The famous Wistaria Lamp with bronze tree trunk base and irregular lower border designed by Mrs Curtis Freshell of Tiffany Studios. Over 1000 pieces of coloured glass are skilfully worked into the shade design.**

LEFT: This double gourd
vase was made in the
1890s. Inspiration for the
shape is drawn from
antiquity, but the design
of surging contour lines is
essentially Art Nouveau.

confidence exceeded his artistry, sometimes the tastes of his clients dictated a banal 19th-century sentimentality that finds no favour today.

He was at his best when suggesting a subject, a theme, a scene, a flower, in the impressionistic, romantic, Art Nouveau style.

Favrile glass, with its strange, integral, iridescent colours and marbled designs, its curious free-form shapes, smooth, and sinuous and uncluttered with decoration, was the most beautiful glass of its era. Essentially, it was in the spirit of Art Nouveau. Inspired by the finest glass of the past, Roman, Persian and Venetian, it has come to take its place beside them.

In the vases Tiffany turned to natural forms for inspiration and interpreted them in glass: strange swirling patterns and flowers are trapped as if by magic in the glass; slender vases are like petals half opened, like buds unfolding. Form, material, colour and light were used in such a way that each enhanced the other, without external decoration being added.

The lamps evolved in the 1890s, using excess glass from the windows and the same techniques. The decision to produce them might have been purely commercial to begin with, but the combination of the beauty of Favrile glass and the inspiration drawn from nature meant that Tiffany and his team of craftsmen at Tiffany Studios produced lamps that have continued to delight ever since. There is real joy in looking at these lamps. They are visually pleasing, graceful and vibrantly colourful, the leaded shades give a soft, diffused quality to the light. They epitomize the Art Nouveau unity of form, with glass shades representing the blossoms of wistaria, magnolia, lotus or laburnam, bronze stems representing the trunk and the base, roots spread into the earth. All the Tiffany favourite themes appear in lamps: peacock feathers, dragonflies, lilies, spider's webs.

Tiffany Studios' output of lamps and Favrile glass vases was prodigious. Tiffany's popularity was enormous and classless in its appeal. While his designs for interiors were much in demand by the wealthy, and were awarded the ultimate accolade of a commission for the president and the White House, his declared goal was to bring beauty into every home so that everyone might experience it, absorb its substance and so enhance their lives. Soon no house was complete without a Tiffany lamp, at least one Favrile glass vase and stained glass over the front door.

Even at the height of his fame, though, there were critical voices. Was his skill as an artist, innovator and creative genius being overtaken by his commercial sense? Inevitably, there were times when he stumbled, as every innovator must, but could such a huge output really maintain quality of the highest order?

Other critics have seen qualities of the quattrocento in his vast energy, vitality and versatility, his technical discoveries and scientific concerns, his mastery of so many branches of the arts. The organization of the workshops of Tiffany Studios has been likened to the Florentine *bottegas.* Tuscan artists could be sculptors, painters, goldsmiths, designers and decorators, in the way that Tiffany was decorator and architect, painter in oil and watercolour, designer, creator, skilled and original maker of beautiful glass.

He himself was proud of his ranging talents, never limiting his curiosity as an artist to one or two paths of art, following first one road then another, never allowing himself to be restricted by the old traditions and accepted formulas, turning to stained glass, mosaic, pottery, enamels, tapestries, jewellery, furniture, landscape and house design.

For 40 years Tiffany was the leader, the outstanding fashionable artist and the success story of American Art Nouveau. At the turn of the century he was producing a vast range for the American and foreign markets, employing 100 craftsmen and maintaining at all times his personal involvement.

But Art Nouveau, which had been such a liberating influence, was abruptly dropped by artists and patrons in the early years of the new century. It could not survive the harsh realities of the First World War. Tiffany was appalled at the stark functionalism that succeeded it. He lived to see Tiffany Studios fade away, producing merely wedding presents and gifts. His last years were full of disappointment and neglect; much of his work was lost or ignored. The glass screen at the White House, commissioned by President Arthur at the height of Tiffany's fame, was destroyed on the instruction of President Theodore Roosevelt, who hated it.

Many years passed before Tiffany and Favrile glass were rediscovered and it was realized that the creativity and inventiveness of the Art Nouveau artists had more poetic imagination, than anything produced during the succeeding 50 years.

RIGHT: **Favrile**
**paperweight vases are**
**rare and costly. They were**
**made by encasing a richly**
**decorated layer of glass in**
**a smooth outer layer so**
**that the decoration of**
**flowers appears trapped**
**in the glass itself. The**
**name refers to the use of**
**a similar technique used**
**in the manufacture of**
**French paperweights.**

In the 1950s Robert Koch of Yale University researching for his doctorate, discovered that Tiffany had decorated the Veterans' Room and Library of an armoury building in New York City. Becoming fascinated by the artist, he set about writing a study of Louis Comfort Tiffany, and purchased for $4 a Favrile vase. At that time it was difficult to locate Tiffany work anywhere, but once interest was aroused, notable items appeared. Many were acquired by museums and there was a Tiffany exhibition at the Museum of Contemporary Crafts in New York in 1958. Tiffany items soon multiplied in value. Since then the prices of some lamps and vases have risen as much as one hundred times. A Favrile vase sold for a mere $20 in the 1940s could fetch $80,000 today, and a record price of $528,000 was paid at a sale at Christie's, New York, in March 1985 for a magnolia lamp by Tiffany.

It is a dramatic story, full of vitality and glamour, of a man convinced of his own genius, adventurous and confident enough to be unorthodox; a man with advantages and the talent to pursue his own artistic aims and to achieve greatness; a man who has been ignored and then vindicated by time.

# PRIVILEGED REBEL

"What I've found does the most good is just to get in a taxi and go to Tiffany's. It calms me down right away, the quietness and the proud look of it; nothing bad could happen to you there, not with those kind men in nice suits, and that lovely smell of silver and aligator wallets."

HOLLY GOLIGHTLY

THE MAN WHO STARTED IT all, Charles Lewis Tiffany, was born in Connecticut in 1812, the son of a prosperous textile maker. The family could trace its ancestry to Squire Humphrey Tiffany, who settled in Massachusetts Bay Colony around 1660. Perhaps it was from these New England ancestors that the famous Tiffanys, father and son, inherited the great advantages of physical and moral strength, determined energy and capacity for work.

Charles Tiffany gained business experience at an early age, working in his father's textile mill, managing his general store in Connecticut and occasionally making buying trips to New York City. In 1837, when he was 25, he borrowed $1,000 from his father and invested in a small stationery and fancy goods store with a partner, John B. Young.

The store that was to become the internationally famous jewellery store began life as Tiffany and Young on Broadway, opposite City Hall Park. The times were not prosperous: there was a great deal of unemployment, many had been ruined by the business panic of that year and New York still bore the scars of a great fire of two years before.

Receipts on the first day totalled only $4.98. But the business went rapidly from strength to strength. Charles Tiffany, it has been said, was a man born to sell. He courted a mass market with "Useful and Fancy Articles", bronze statuettes, Japanese lacquerware, cutlery, toiletries, Tiffany Timer stopwatches, Chinese umbrellas, fans and curiosities, Venetian glass writing implements, "seegar" boxes, American Indian artefacts. He had a gift for anticipating popular taste and recognized the appeal of novelty.

At first gems were promoted only as "best quality imitation jewelry", but by 1841 Tiffany and Young were buying the real thing in Europe, proudly describing themselves as the only store in New York with a representative abroad.

That representative was John Young and he was in Paris for his annual buying trip in 1848, when revolution broke out against King Louis Philippe. Mobs were looting the vaults of the Palace of the Tuileries; aristocrats were taking flight and dumping their jewels on the market. The price of diamonds dropped by half, and Charles Tiffany was ready to buy.

Laden with jewels, John Young was arrested as a Royalist plotter and had to talk himself out of trouble to avoid the firing squad. Afterwards it was Charles Tiffany who talked to great effect about John Young's exploits in Paris, making the most of

the publicity, and it was Charles Tiffany who gained the name King of Diamonds.

Two years later Tiffany's opened a Paris branch, which soon established itself well ahead of its New York rivals. They bought diamonds from the fabulous collection of the Hungarian Prince Esterhazy and acquired Marie Antoinette's girdle of diamonds in some mysterious way, breaking it up so that it was not recognized in order to sell it.

Charles Tiffany bought a huge and perfect pink pearl from a New Jersey farmer who had found it among his mussels at dinner and resold it to the Empress Eugénie of France, then reigning with Napoleon III over the glittering Second Empire. Later, when the Empire fell, Tiffany's would buy the French crown jewels, including the former Empress's great necklace of 222 diamonds in four rows, at auction. The necklace next appeared in public, said one newspaper commentator, "at a ball, on the handsome neck and shoulders of Mrs Joseph Pulitzer".

Many of the European monarchies were shaky and Tiffany's acted as middlemen, buying from kings and queens and selling to millionaires. Gems worth $1.6 million, purchased from the deposed Queen Isabella of Spain, were sold to the wife of the railroad tycoon Leland Stanford.

With his financial strength and his ability to make a quick decision, Charles Tiffany could take advantage of bargains and opportunities wherever they occurred. Anyone finding gems or wanting to sell them was rewarded with a prompt cheque.

In 1877 the Tiffany Diamond was found in South Africa. It weighed 128.51 carats and was purchased for $18,000.

Tiffany's never became a store for the super-rich alone. Their democratic attitude of treating every customer equally made them a very American symbol of luxury, something everyone could aspire to. Items for the average income were always stocked, novelties and curios from the Far East were imported. Charles Tiffany was one of the first to look beyond Europe, and Japanese arts in particular caught American imagination.

From the beginning the store sponsored American craftsmanship and established Tiffany silverware by hiring the best known silversmith in New York, John C. Moore, to work exclusively for them. American silver at Tiffany's came, under Charles Tiffany's instructions, to match the purity of English sterling and set the standard of 925 parts silver per 1,000, with a trace of copper for durability and strength.

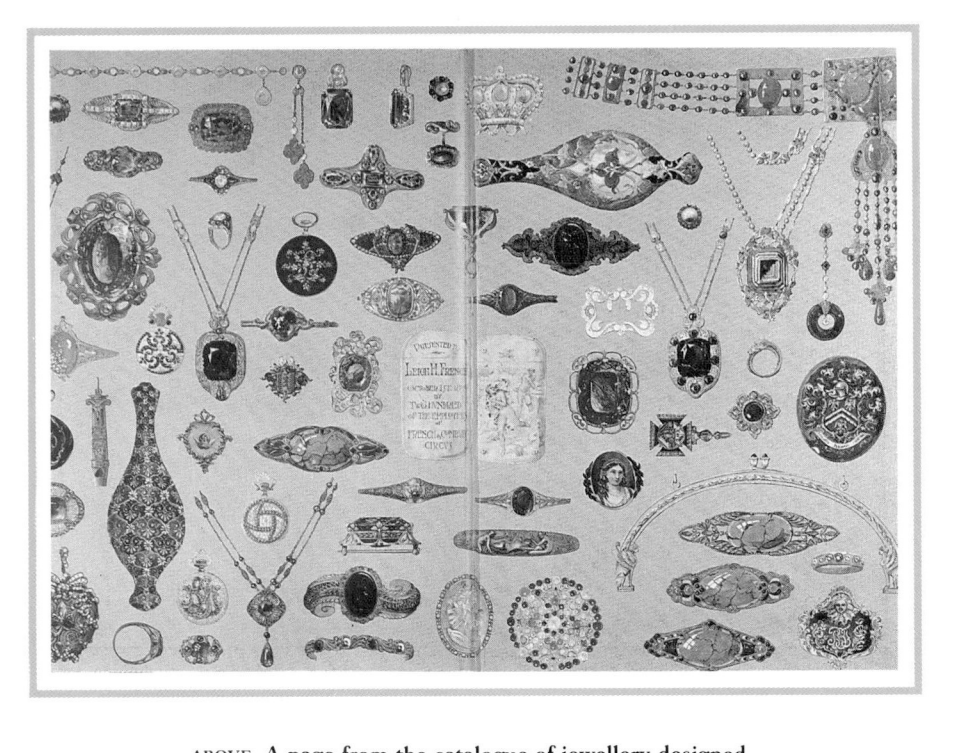

ABOVE: A page from the catalogue of jewellery designed by Tiffany & Co, New York c.1890. The store was internationally famous by this time, catering for the crowned heads of Europe and the new American millionaires but also a democratic symbol of luxury, somewhere everyone could aspire to visit.

RIGHT: Necklace of diamonds and enamelled gilt by Tiffany & Co, New York 1870.

When John Moore retired, his son Edward C. Moore succeeded him and brought the store international fame for its silver over 40 years. The Tiffany silver workshops grew from employing a mere handful of artisans to 500, and new mechanized processes were adopted.

Moore's elegant silver tea set won a prize at the 1867 Paris Exposition, the first time an American silver company had been honoured by a foreign jury. In the 1878 Exposition, he won the Gold Medal. European silver houses bought his pieces as patterns for their own ware.

Edward Moore played a very influential role among the artists and craftsmen in New York all his life. Samuel Bing said of him: "His country should forever shrine him in grateful memory", for he set new high standards for *objets d'art* in America, and he was a man of great knowledge and sophisticated appreciation. He introduced many artists to Persian and Islamic art, their geometric abstractions and intricate designs. He was one of the first to appreciate Japanese art and Japanese skills in metals, developing a style of his own based on Japanese and Moorish models. His work and his fine collection of Oriental and antique glass had a great influence on the artistic development of Louis Comfort Tiffany.

Tiffany's brought a kind of civilizing zeal to retailing, taking it upon themselves to improve manners and style along with design. Tiffany's disdained fashion and the view that the customer is always right, refusing to sell items they considered tasteless and pretentious, such as a man's diamond ring.

Tiffany and Young became Tiffany & Co when John Young retired and moved uptown to 550 Broadway, where a carved wooden Atlas held aloft a huge clock above the door. This clock moved with the firm to three other locations and today oversees the store's Fifth Avenue entrance. New Yorkers still recall the legend that the clock stopped at the exact moment of Abraham Lincoln's death: 7.22 am on 15 April, 1865.

Louis Comfort Tiffany was born into this exceptional setting of culture and commerce, art and enterprise. He grew up surrounded by rare and beautiful things, learning from them throughout his formative years. He realized the great advantage this gave him and in later life sought to give others a similar aesthetic experience in their homes.

He was born on 18 February, 1848, the year of the revolutionary upheavals in Europe that gave his father his great opportunity to acquire diamonds in Paris. His

mother Harriet, was the sister of Charles's partner, John Young, and the daughter of Judge Ebenezer Young of Connecticut. She had planned to raise her children on strictly Congregational principles, combining common sense and severity, she did not believe in spoiling children. Louis was her third son; she had lost her first child when he was in his fourth year and her second before he was a year old. Perhaps for this reason, and partly because Louis was a dreamy, moody child, her stern theories seem to have been defeated in practice.

While Louis Tiffany has said in *The Artwork of Louis Comfort Tiffany*, the book recording his achievements, that he "was born with a golden spoon in his mouth", he also went on to say that "the spoon was immediately tucked away and he was seldom permitted to remember its existence."

For Louis and his younger brother, Burnett and his two sisters, Annie and Louise, education was thorough, luxuries were few and spending money was curtailed. The family regularly attended the Congregational Church. As the eldest son, Louis was intended to continue the family tradition, taking over the flourishing firm of Tiffany & Co in due course.

However, from early on it became clear that Louis's nature was unpredictable and mercurial, with great energy, ingenuity and bursts of creative talent when he was interested in something coupled with capricious moods and a disruptive wilfulness. He showed little interest in school work when he was sent to boarding school, Flushing Academy on Long Island, and then to a military academy. There his interests are recorded as wandering the beach collecting bits of coloured glass and pebbles worn into curious shapes by the sea.

It was the time of the Civil War. Tiffany & Co supplied swords, epaulettes and other military paraphernalia. At the outbreak of war Charles Tiffany converted his elegant showrooms into a depot for military supplies, advertising "swords from Solingen Passants; cap ornaments ... from Paris, gold epaulettes ... from London". Tiffany & Co made and supplied swords, boots, caps, rifles, medals, badges, even ambulances. The state of Ohio alone ordered 20,000 cap badges, and Charles Tiffany amassed a fortune.

Louis Tiffany left school as the Civil War ended, with no ambitions for military glory or for commerce. He declared that he wanted to be an artist. Charles Tiffany seems to have accepted his son's rebellious nature and allowed him to choose his own path. There was a strong bond of affection between father and son, as both

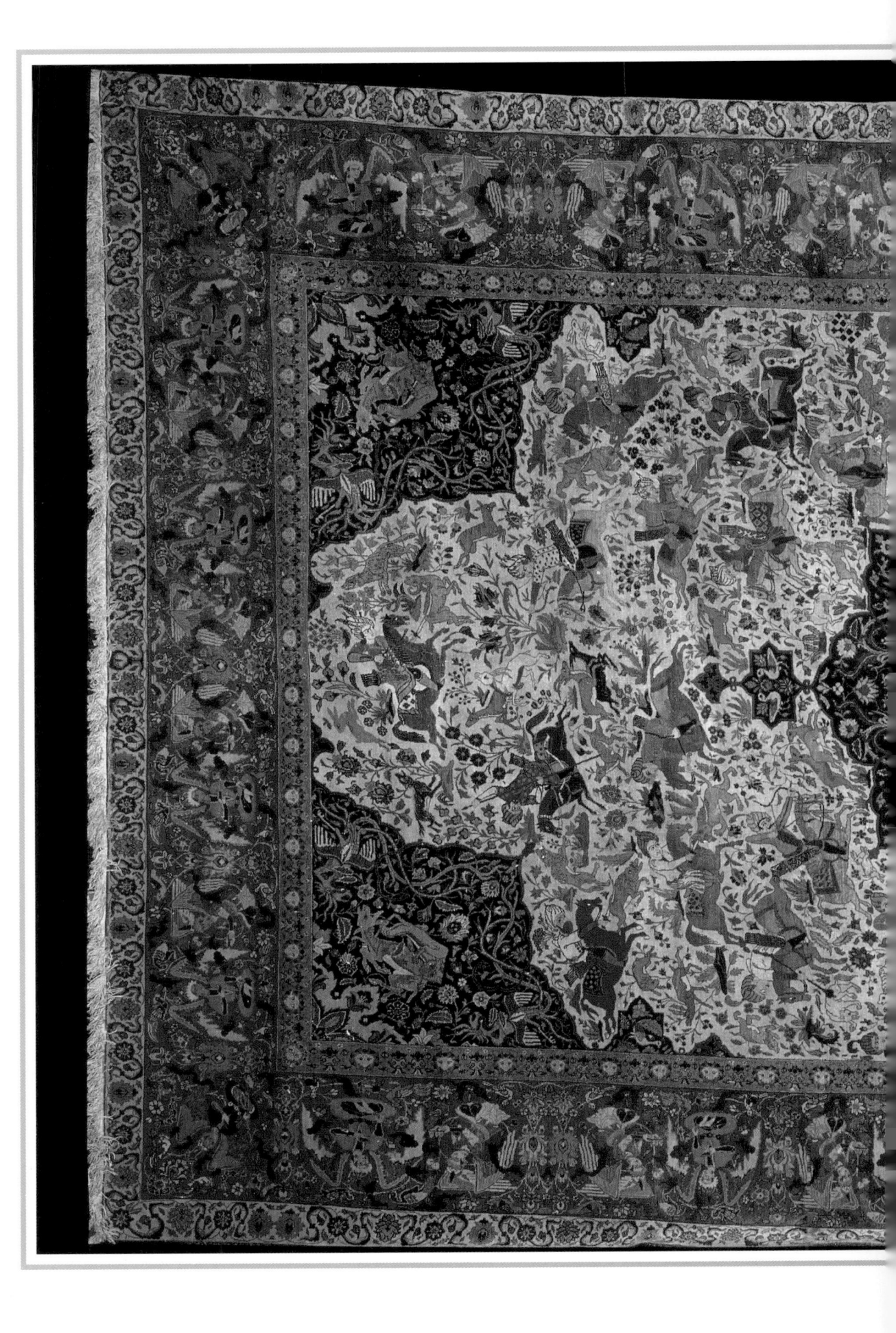

RIGHT: Louis Tiffany's travels in the Middle East opened his eyes to another world of colour and design. Middle Eastern designs and crafts such as this Tabriz carpet became a notable feature of his exotic interior designs.

shared an appreciation of beautiful things, and Charles Tiffany understood that his son was talented and determined. He let him have his chance rather than force him into the jewellery store to learn the business, a role which many successful self-made men of that time forced on their sons.

Louis Tiffany, while rejecting the commercial life and seeking his own way to fame, came in due course to appreciate the strengths of his father's empire, his knowledge and his contacts, and the family bond always remained strong.

Typically, he began his career as an artist by joining a painter at work, George Inness, not by attending classes. Soon he was roaming Manhattan, sketching and throwing himself wholeheartedly into his work in a very serious and hard-working way.

George Inness was working in the style of the Barbizon school of French painters, Jean François Millet, Théodore Rousseau and Narcisse Virgile Diaz. They were beginning to bring a new sense of the landscape into their paintings with light and shadow and movement, and Inness was introducing a kind of unprettified realism to American painting that was vivid and atmospheric.

By the following year, 1867, Tiffany, a 19-year-old, exhibited a painting at the National Academy of Design.

At Inness's studios there were gatherings of young men with wide-ranging interests. There Tiffany met James Steel MacKaye, the playwright, who later introduced him to the Aesthetic Movement, begun by the painter James McNeill Whistler, with Oscar Wilde as its most flamboyant exponent. Wilde later made a highly publicized and provocative lecture tour haranguing America on such subjects as The English Renaissance, The House Beautiful and The Decorative Arts. In this he was developing themes that had already found favour in America with the ideas of William Morris and the Arts and Crafts Movement.

This was the beginning of a new movement which refused to accept the cult of the past and wanted to break free of academic traditions, and the movement was taking shape all over Europe.

Louis Tiffany found many of his half-formed ideas developed in this way. He responded to the Arts and Crafts Movement's dedication to craftsman-

ship and the turning to nature for inspiration. He was in sympathy with many of the beliefs of the Aesthetic Movement. Oscar Wilde talked of bringing artist and craftsman together, bringing art into everyday life, bringing colour into the home. Tiffany was to work towards those aims throughout his life. Wilde declared that comely surroundings could foster a fuller existence, that growing up with ugly wallpaper could lead a boy to a life of crime. He brought his lectures to a rousing finale: "We spend our days looking for the secret of life. Well, the secret of life is art."

These were exciting times to be an artist. No wonder Tiffany declared that the life of an artist was the "only one" for him. In 1868 he set off for Paris. By this time Charles Tiffany had a branch there, another in London and a watch-making factory in Geneva. Louis Tiffany's trip was in part like the Grand Tour undertaken by the sons of wealthy families to complete their education, in part a business trip making contact with his father's European connections, but above all learning as an art student.

He worked in Paris with the French artist Léon Bailly, in the same informal way he had worked with George Inness. Bailly had travelled widely in North Africa and Palestine, and had exhibited paintings of Islamic landscapes. He opened the door for Tiffany to another culture, another world of pattern and colour.

Tiffany already had an appreciation of Oriental arts and a knowledge of the exotic Eastern crafts. He responded at once to this new stimulus. The Middle Eastern styles that were to be such a notable feature of Tiffany's exotic interior designs had their birthplace here and were greatly influenced by the Moorish decorations of Spain.

Travelling first to Spain, he met Samuel Colman, an American artist also travelling and studying, who became a close friend and business associate. Samuel Colman was a watercolourist and from him Tiffany first learned to work in the watercolour medium, preserving his immediate impressions of form and colour. While Colman's interest was aroused particularly by Islamic textiles, Tiffany was excited by the architecture, and his love of detail begins to emerge in his paintings from this time.

With no anxieties about finances or future security, Tiffany was able to travel freely for a couple of years in Europe, the Middle East and North

Africa. These visits made a strong impression on him and his creative development. He said later: "When I first had a chance to travel in the East and to paint where the people and buildings also are clad in beautiful hues, the pre-eminence of color in the world was brought forcibly to my attention. I returned to New York wondering why we made so little use of our eyes, why we refrained so obstinately from taking advantage of color in our architecture and our clothing."

Visiting London at that time, Tiffany found the Aesthetic Movement in full swing. Then and on later visits he would have seen the progress of Whistler's Peacock Room, which had such a crucial influence on the development of interior decoration — and on Tiffany's style.

The Peacock Room Whistler created between 1867 and 1877 for a house in Princes Gate was the outstanding example of an artist disregarding the barrier between fine art and applied art. He was undertaking interior design, creating a room as a whole, with a peacock theme, which was to become a recurring motif.

It is also interesting to note that at about this time Arthur Lazenby Liberty was manager of the Oriental Warehouse in Regent Street and in 1875 he opened his own shop. The London branch of Tiffany & Co opened in London at 221 Regent Street in 1868, the year Tiffany went to Europe, and there is a fascinating resemblance between the two companies.

Like Tiffany's, Arthur Liberty began selling *objets d'art* from Japan and the East to cater for current fashion. He soon expanded to include fabrics, carpets, china and glass. His customers included Morris, Burne-Jones, Rossetti, Whistler and Wilde. He patronized and encouraged artists and craftsmen, as Charles Tiffany did in New York, in a wide range of new designs in silver, pewter, gemstones and enamel and he also did pioneering work in furniture design, fabrics, wallpapers and glass, as Louis Tiffany was to do subsequently.

The London fashion scene was divided into two camps: the languid and foppish aesthetes and the old guard of Victorian philistines, happy with sentimentality and fake neo-classicism.

The aesthetes were attacked, parodied and satirized, most memorably in the Gilbert and Sullivan opera *Patience.*

RIGHT:c
 Roman and Syrian blown glass of
the 1st Century AD was being
unearthed by archaeologists at the
time Louis Tiffany visited Europe.
He was deeply impressed by the
technical achievement of these
ancient civilizations and by the
way the colour of the glass —
buried for centuries — had
acquired a soft and pearly sheen.

A Japanese young man
A blue and white young man
Francesca di Rimini, niminy-piminy
Je-ne-sais-quoi young man

A pallid and thin young man
A haggard and lank young man
A greenery-yallery, Grosvenor Gallery,
Foot-in-the-grave young man.

At the Grosvenor Gallery exhibition Whistler had exhibited his painting *Nocturnes in Black and Gold — the Falling Rocket*, described as "a rhymically formless ornament". Ruskin accused the artist of "flinging a pot of paint in the face of the public"; Whistler then sued Ruskin and was awarded a farthing damages. The greenery-yallery reference is to Liberty's Umritza Cashmere colour. The blue and white young man mocks Wilde's well-known remark that he was a young man whose greatest difficulty in life was living up to the level of his blue and white china.

Out of the Arts and Crafts Movement and the Aesthetic Movement a trend that was to become even more important in Tiffany's career was about to emerge. It was developing first of all in France, where there was no special interest in the teachings of Ruskin and Morris.

The term Art Nouveau was first coined by Octave Maus and Edmond Picard when they created the review *L'Art Moderne* in 1881. At first it was applied to the work of painters who were rejecting the old academic traditions and producing their own revolutionary style. Later, when the painters were given other impressionist labels, the term was extended to architecture and art objects.

Different countries would, by the end of the century, produce their own versions: in England there was Liberty style; in America Tiffany would reign supreme. With strong anti-academic feelings, and rejection of slavish devotion to the classical tradition and its straight lines, went a new observation and imitation of nature, with lines curved and colours cleared and brightened

ABOVE: *On the Way between Old and New Cairo, Citadel Mosque of Mohammed Ali and the Tombs of the Mamelukes.* Oil on canvas painted by Louis Tiffany c.1872 following his travels in North Africa and already showing his strength as a colourist.

ABOVE: *Duane Street, New York,* painted by Louis Tiffany in
1875, showed his bold originality in its contemporary
realism, anticipating the American Ashcan School of
painting.

boldly. For many of the exponents of the new art, these exciting developments went with democratic ideals and sympathy with the socialist cause.

Tiffany had the opportunity on his travels of seeing the great stained-glass windows in the medieval cathedrals of Europe and his admiration for these was heightened by his fascination with glass as a medium.

Antiquity held the beginnings of glass. He was deeply impressed by the qualities of the Roman and Syrian glass of the 1st century AD which was being unearthed by archaeologists at the time. Ancient glass was astonishing the world: that civilizations so far back in time could have produced such astounding shapes and colours was a revelation, and Tiffany was fascinated by the technical achievement. Many of the glass objects, buried for centuries, had been affected by metallic oxides in the soil and these had given the glass surfaces a pearly, iridescent sheen. Each object was complete in itself, without etching or painting, and that appealed to Tiffany strongly.

The art of working in coloured glass had been known for centuries. The glowing, jewel-bright stained-glass windows of the cathedrals, where mosaics of broken colours were put together with lead, were evidence enough. The colour was in the glass, with each piece a single colour, and special effects were achieved by juxtaposition of pieces to denote shading, drapery and so on. The glass was of unequal thickness, sometimes filled with air bubbles, all of which added to the brilliance and translucency.

The high point of the craft was in the 14th century and there had been a decline since the Renaissance. Once painters began to work on the walls and windows of churches, the translucency of the glass was spoiled. The glassworkers' art was lost, the glorious reds and glowing blues had long gone.

It was time to go back to the beginning, to learn the art anew, and already in England Tiffany may have seen the work of William Morris and Company. Burne-Jones designed windows for Morris from 1861, designs which were made up of a number of small pieces of glass of various colours, etching into the glass with metallic oxides.

Tiffany had travelled to widen his experience as a painter, but he learned so much more that it fired his creative work throughout his career.

On his return to America he first concentrated on his work as a painter and in 1870 became the youngest member ever to be elected to the Century

Club. The following year he was an associate member of the National Academy of Design and in 1880, a full member. His paintings are interesting, in view of his later career, for their strength of colour. He believed that line and form were of secondary importance — they disappeared at a short distance, while colour remained visible for much longer. He began to use painting techniques closer to those of the Impressionists. He was determined to break away from the dim browns and turgid tones of the past; leaves in his paintings were realistically green and flesh tones were so fleshy that they provoked acrimonious comment from the critics on his audacity. He drew inspiration from nature, but not as a slavish copyist. He said of flowers: "Their form is distinctly a secondary consideration which comes after the satisfaction we feel in their color."

It was because he felt constricted by the narrow views of the National Academy that Tiffany became a founder member of the Society of American Artists, which had a broader view of art.

His obsession with colour and decoration found expression in his Oriental works: *Mosque and Market Place, Ruins of Tangiers, Citadel of Cairo* and *View of the Nile.* In *The Snake Charmer at Tangiers* the effect is achieved with the rich colours of the carpet, the Arab clothing of the group of people watching and the intricate basketwork, all set against the brilliant light on tall pillars, roof tiles and high desert sky.

In his Oriental pictures Tiffany shows the influence of his travels and his teachers, in his urban studies he shows his bold originality. He was well ahead of his time when he painted *Duane Street, New York,* anticipating the American Ashcan School in aiming to found an American art based on a realistic portrayal of the contemporary scene.

Tiffany was working at that time in a rented studio at the YMCA, which was well placed across the road from the National Academy of Design, and he was part of a group of artists which included George Inness, John La Farge and Samuel Colman.

He is described at this stage in his life as a "live wire ... never still" and "he never missed a trick". He does not seem to have been a great talker, nor was he given to philosophizing, to abstract ideas or writing; he expressed himself through art.

RIGHT: Stone-set silver vase, a showpiece designed for the Paris Exposition of 1900 by Tiffany & Co, New York. Charles Tiffany and his silversmith Edward C. Moore set new standards of quality and design for American craftsmanship and won many international awards.

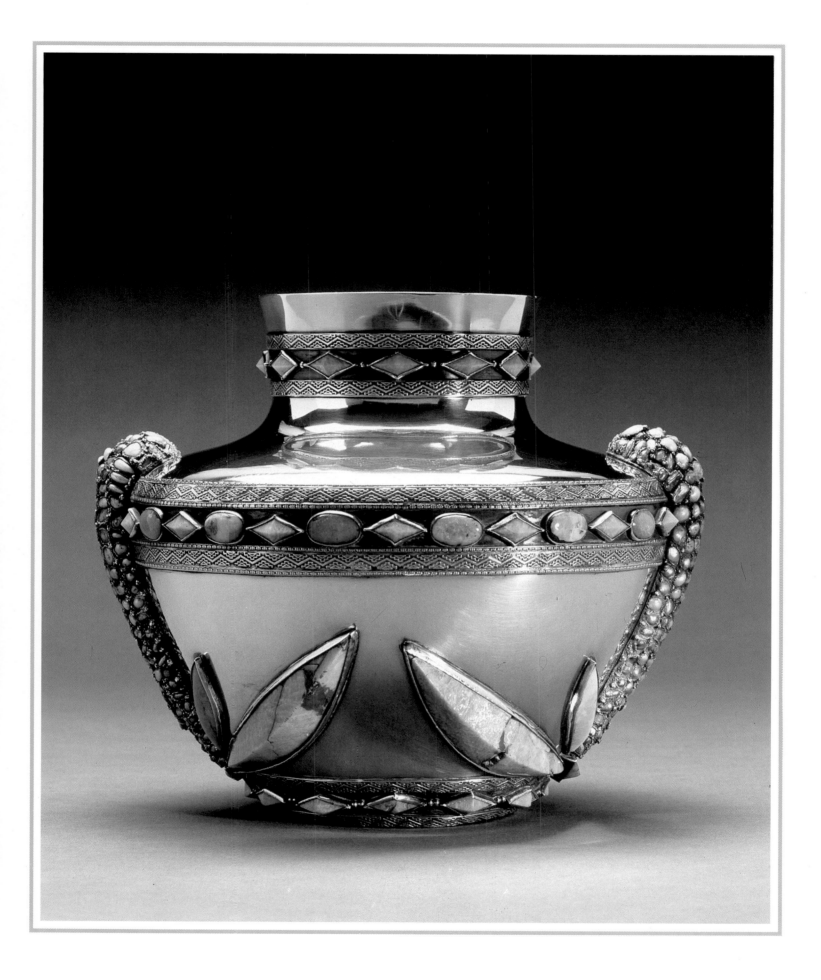

He appears in photographs and his own self-portrait as a dark, good-looking young man with fine eyes, straight heavy brows, a sensuous mouth and a determined chin. He seems to have been popular, though he was moody at times and could be overbearing.

He was evidently popular with Mary Woodbridge Goddard, and they married in 1872. She shared his love of nature, appearing in photographs and his paintings walking in the fields and gathering blossom with their children. She seems to have shared Tiffany's confidence in his abilities and responded to his moods and enthusiasms.

Their first daughter was born in 1873 and there are happy pictures of the family on a painting holiday in Brittany the following year.

There is no mention of his wife in Tiffany's book, which is really devoted to his work, but it is known that she was delicate. In 1874 she had a son, who lived only three weeks. Her health was impaired and she never fully recovered, contracting tuberculosis.

In 1878 their son Charles, was born and they moved into an apartment at 48 East Street, New York, spending their summer holidays on Charles Tiffany's estate in Irvington-on-Hudson. A second daughter was born in 1879.

Tiffany continued to paint all through his career, deriving great pleasure from it, but it was becoming clear that painting was not enough to express his great creative force. Perhaps, too, as a perfectionist, Tiffany was aware that his painting was not of the highest order — good, but not good enough to satisfy him.

Many influences in his life came together to direct him into the wider fields of applied arts. In 1876 a turning-point was the Philadelphia Centennial Exposition. Tiffany exhibited nine paintings, but what fascinated him most were the examples of applied arts. At the Exposition could be seen on display the nation's progress in trade, manufacture and decorative arts, and the cultural exchange between the United States and Europe.

Here Tiffany saw again the developments of the Arts and Crafts Movement that he had encountered in England, such as wallpaper designed by Walter Crane and a beautiful screen of embroidered peacocks from the Royal School of Art Needlework. This example of applied art deeply impressed Samuel Colman, who had a great collection of textiles, and Candace

RIGHT: **An iridescent glass vase on a silver stand, 1897. Louis Tiffany's discovery and development of richly coloured glass is combined with the sculptured silver of his father's firm Tiffany & Co, New York.**

Tiffany had a vision of rooms rich with colour ornate detail, sumptuous textures, glowing glass. Two of the earliest interior design commissions for Louis C. Tiffany & Associated Artists were the parlour at No 8 Fifth Avenue for Mr J. Taylor Johnston (ABOVE) and the dining room at 47 East 34th street for Dr William T. Lusk with a bronze frieze and transoms of amber glass (BELOW).

Wheeler, herself a master of embroidery whose interests extended to all branches of design. She was impressed by the idea that the Royal School of Art Needlework provided profitable work for impoverished gentlewomen in England and was determined that the same should be done in America. To this end she enlisted the support of Samuel Colman and formed the Society of Decorative Art in New York, inviting Tiffany to become involved, lecturing on painting and pottery.

Very soon this was not enough to satisfy Tiffany — too much talk about art made him impatient — but it brought him to an important decision. He told Mrs Wheeler: "I have been thinking a great deal about decorative work, and I am going into it as a profession. I believe there is more in it than in painting pictures."

He was so sure of this that he immediately formed Louis C. Tiffany and Associated Artists, with Candace Wheeler and Samuel Colman as partners, and began a new career as an interior designer.

Tiffany was exceptionally well placed to launch the company, since his father's business contacts meant he had connections with the right market — the wealthy American elite. America was flourishing, and its industrial and commercial prosperity had created families with great wealth who were eager to spend it, to make clear to the world their status and income. They were "extravagant people leading extravagant lives" and for them the new company created homes of exotic magnificence. Very soon the word spread among this privileged group and there was praise for the "harmonized" schemes for rooms, the originality of the designs and the high quality of the workmanship.

Tiffany had a vision of rooms rich with colour, ornate detail, sumptuous textures and glowing glass. The style of decoration had its inspiration in Byzantine, Islamic richness and in the famous Peacock Room of Whistler. It appealed to the taste of the first patrons, many of them nouveau riche, who felt that in this rich setting, with a wealth of *objets d'art* displayed, they were clearly demonstrating their importance.

During these years Tiffany was developing his personal style. He was often impatient with the restrictions and the traditional taste of his clients; he was startling and original with his brilliant colours, glass tiles and the stained-

glass windows he introduced into interior settings. He was soon noted as an outstanding colourist. He designed wallpapers and at once achieved an original, individual look. One Tiffany paper was a snowflake pattern printed in black on gold, refined and Islamic and interlaced, that has his signature on it.

His taste in interior design was close to the theatrical, its exotic boldness and strong colours contrasting with the quieter tastes of Candace Wheeler and the textiles and embroideries she favoured. It was difficult for Tiffany to be part of a team, but a team was needed to carry out the first, prestigious commissions — for George Kemp on Fifth Avenue and for one of the public rooms of the new Seventh Regiment Armory on Park Avenue. One of the earliest commissions was the design of the drop-curtain at the Madison Square Theater, which was to open in February 1880 with a play written by Tiffany's friend James Steel MacKaye. The newspapers noted that instead of calling in conventional designers, MacKaye had secured the aid of Louis C. Tiffany and "as a result we have a revelation of beauty".

The drop-curtain was an experiment in new methods of appliqué, combining free use of paint, thread and textiles in a collage, which was then embroidered and painted on a background of velvet and satin. A landscape of oak and birch trees, wistaria and yucca was created in iridescent textiles, with shadowy silks for the misty blue distance.

The curtain was destroyed by fire before the first season ended. Fire was to be a recurring disaster in Tiffany's life, but it was characteristic that the curtain was replaced with an improved copy, one praised by Oscar Wilde when he visited New York.

The Islamic style of Tiffany interiors can be seen in the library designed for Mr W.S. Kimball's home in Rochester, New York with the wide arch over the tiled fireplace and stained glass windows (ABOVE). The drawing room in Stuyvesant Square designed for the Hon Hamilton Fish has the ornate magnificence that displayed the wealth and status of the American elite. It featured a carved mantel, Indian teak panels, a Moorish frieze and peacock blue plush (BELOW).

# COLORIST
# SUPREME

"Color is to the eye as music to the ear"

LOUIS C. TIFFANY

Louis C. Tiffany and Associated Artists very soon made their mark. Tiffany had established his partnership with Candace Wheeler and Samuel Colman in 1879 and little more than a year later their work was being praised by the critics. "Perhaps the broadest most original and richest development yet seen in America," one prestigious magazine on interior design noted. "the little band of associated artists headed by Mr Louis C. Tiffany, have only recently established an atelier in New York. Their work is as yet little known to the general public, and has been executed chiefly for luxurious interiors intended to show every detail harmonized according to the highest standards of decorative art."

Other critics noted that the team's work for the Madison Square Theater "is decorated with that sense of color and harmony that go into a great painting".

The successful businessmen of the day were commissioning lavish buildings for their homes and businesses, often massive buildings designed to impress. Tiffany was one of the first to understand the link that must be made between architecture and interior design. Instead of the hotch-potch of rich objects that were currently displayed in rooms to indicate status and wealth, he believed that each room should have its own theme.

The interiors designed by Associated Artists had an exotic, Islamic feel and immediately showed Tiffany's love of opulent colour, intricate detail and stained glass. They quickly developed a fashionable magnificence.

The first complete interior was executed for the home of George Kemp on Fifth Avenue and had an Oriental, interlaced ceiling with hanging lamps and a frieze painted by Louis Tiffany. Tiffany lined the fireplace with his own glass tiles and put panels of opalescent glass in the transoms above the doors.

One of the early commissions for a public building was for the Veterans' Room of the Seventh Regiment Armory. Their design expressed the idea of the war veteran with materials and decorations "undeniably assimilable and matchable with the huge hard, clanging ponderosities of wars and tramping regiments". There were ponderous soffit beams, with axe-cuts showing on them, metallic lustres, iron decorations, a large fireplace framed by Tiffany with glass tiles, and over the mantel, framed in hammered iron, was a plaque representing a struggle between a dragon and an eagle. High oaken wainscotting was surmounted with carving of Japanese inspiration and there were rectangular bolted panels, Celtic interlaced ornaments and wrought-iron chandeliers. The colours were the dark browns of iron, leather

ABOVE: Louis C. Tiffany and Associated Artists' design
for the Veterans Room of the Seventh Regiment Armory
expressed the idea of the war veteran with heavy beams,
oak wainscotting, metallic lustres, wrought iron and
leather combined with Tiffany glass-tiled fireplace and
glass mosaics.

ABOVE TOP: The luxurious interiors designed by Tiffany had every detail harmonized to a theme. The Islamic style was developed with richly coloured rugs and carpets, curving arches, freizes and hanging lamps.

ABOVE BOTTOM: Glass tiles and stained glass featured in the decoration of Mark Twain's home in Hartford, Connecticut, with a window above the dining-room fireplace so that the author could sit indoors by the fire and watch the snow falling.

RIGHT: The bold and colourful effect of Tiffany's design can be seen in this hall and staircase with its detailed lattice work and Islamic friezes.

and oak, lit by translucent glass mosaics suspended in front of the large windows. Glass tiles and a stained glass window featured in the redecoration of Mark Twain's home in Hartford, Connecticut, where Tiffany placed a window above the dining room fireplace at the author's suggestion, so that "he could watch the flames leap to reach the falling snowflakes". Stencilled decorations designed after Indian motifs were added to ceiling and walls and Tiffany supplied amber, turquoise and brown tiles in transparent and opalescent glass. Mark Twain was happy to say: "The work is not merely and coldly satisfactory but intensely so."

In 1881 two elaborate and troublesome schemes were undertaken at the same time by Associated Artists. A commission to redecorate the home of Ogden Goelet at 59th Street and Fifth Avenue was completed first for a fee of more than $50,000. The decoration of the Vanderbilt mansion at 58th Street and Fifth Avenue began with Tiffany's scheme being approved by Cornelius Vanderbilt II with great plea-sure, but more than a year and a half later Candace Wheeler was still coping with the difficulties, being put to great trouble and expense with the job, and reporting: "Mrs Vanderbilt absolutely refused to have the green plush."

LEFT: Mark Twain was intensely pleased with the sumptuous drawing room designed for his mansion in Connecticut by Associated Artists.

ABOVE: An invitation to re-decorate rooms in the White House for President Chester Alan Arthur was a challenge for Tiffany and the ultimate accolade. (top) In the East Room the glass mosaic sconces were highly praised. (below) The crowning achievement was the floor-to-ceiling glass screen of national emblems in brightly coloured panels.

While the Vanderbilt commission was still in progress, Tiffany and Associated Artists' position as the pre-eminent American decorators was confirmed by an invitation to redecorate rooms in the White House.

President Chester Alan Arthur wanted the White House cleaned and renovated before he moved in. He declared that it was like a badly kept barracks. Tiffany certainly changed that with his lavish, ostentatious designs. Some 24 loads of furniture were removed and sold at public auction and the work was completed by Associated Artists in an astonishing time of seven weeks.

It was said that all Washington was impressed and delighted at the transformation. There was particular praise for Tiffany's glass-mosaic sconces in the Blue Room: "Four circular sconces, each having seven gas jets are each provided with a background, or rosette, three feet in diameter, composed of fantastic shapes of coloured glass interspersed with little mirrors, to produce a scintillating effect of great variety and brilliancy, which is enhanced by the pendant drops of iridescent glass affixed to the arms that hold the jets."

The crowning achievement of the scheme was the floor-to-ceiling glass screen Tiffany designed, dividing the hallway from the State Dining Room, separating the inner corridor from the public. It was elaborate and exquisite, with brightly coloured panels featuring national emblems, eagles and flags, and was one of the earliest examples of curving free-forms in glass encased in geometric leading.

Recognition as the leading artistic decorators meant that Associated Artists were in great demand. Their successful blending of richly exotic elements became the height of fashion among the wealthy elite. But very soon Tiffany became irritated by the demands of clients; the problems of matching fabric shades and swatches made him impatient, while the development of glass for stained-glass windows and mosaics fascinated and absorbed him.

In designing the decor for his own rooms on the top floor of the Bella Apartment House at 48 East 26th Street, Tiffany was able to indulge his own taste, unhampered by the demands of clients, and he succeeded there in combining the decorative art of East and West into one harmonious whole. He was able to indulge his preference for abstract designs, ideas that were original and functional, bold but not showy. There were exposed beams reaching high up into the peak of the gable, a lobby lit with an abstract stained-glass window and roof slopes set with thick glass tiles to aid the light from the windows.

RIGHT: The high point of the art of stained glass windows was reached in the 14th century in the great Gothic cathedrals such as Chartres in France. Tiffany was inspired to develop similar glass for stained-glass windows in America.

LEFT: Detail from a window designed by Tiffany — Christ with Little Children — for the Church of St Andrew Kimbolton, Cambridgeshire in 1902.

RIGHT: Detail from a window by Tiffany — The Young David as a Shepherd boy — at the church of St Cuthbert Edinburgh, Scotland.

He describes in *The Art Work of Louis C. Tiffany* how in the library he "treated the fireplace in a novel manner, using the whole width of the chimney breast for shelving for books and bric-a-brac and forming out of iron plates an advanced hearth for wood fires without disturbing the hearth behind. The combination of books and open fireplace was an idea which commends itself to book-lovers, for on those shelves are places for favorite authors and, high above easy reach, shelves for particularly admired bric-a-brac".

This fireplace treatment he originated is one that has found great favour ever since. In the dining room an overmantel painting of a turkey and pumpkins in early American decorative style was a focus of colour for the other decorations in the room, and this is another interior design idea that has been adopted widely since.

Tiffany had begun his experiments in glass making as early as 1872. In the days when he was renting a studio at the YMCA he dabbled in experiments, but he was persuaded to desist when some kind of explosion occurred.

He tried again three years later at Thill's Glasshouse in Brooklyn. He made a close study of medieval stained-glass windows — their design, their colour, their construction — analyzing them minutely, and then he set himself to produce the kind of glass colour he wanted. For Tiffany everything began with the glass: pieces of glass were cut to make up the design, then the leading was carefully threaded round the glass. This was a skilled task, requiring time and patience, but the results were true to the artist's designs and turned out to be much superior to the windows and mosaics which started with the outline in lead, the glass then being fixed into the spaces between, made by his competitors.

Tiffany set up his own glass furnaces in 1878, with a Venetian glass-blower, Andrea Boldoni in charge, and he took advantage of the Italian's knowledge of Venetian glass-blowing. Some early Tiffany vases are said to be influenced quite clearly by mid-19th-century glass from Murano.

This venture was ill-fated. The works burned down twice and Boldoni resigned. But Tiffany learned a great deal in the process and continued his experiments at Heidt Glasshouse, also in Brooklyn, applying for patents for three types of glass in 1880: glass suitable for tiles and mosaics, window glass and glass with a metallic lustre. This was the earliest mention of what was eventually to become the famous Favrile art glass.

RIGHT: **The demand for stained glass windows by Tiffany increased dramatically from 1887 onwards. Figure windows with Biblical themes were the most popular, then landscapes and floral subjects, such as this Trumpet Vine leaded glass window.**

LEFT: Tiffany was attracted to stained-glass window design because of the way colour was enhanced by glass and light. Here in this stained-glass window — Hudson River — designed for the reception room at the home of Melchior S. Beltzhover at Irvington, New York, the colours in the glass achieve an amazing freshness and brilliance.

ABOVE: The Coronation of the Blessed Virgin Mary, a window at Milton Manor, Oxford — another example of the medieval stained glass that inspired Tiffany.

He continued to work at Heidt Glasshouse, trying with new methods to produce a wider variety of colour and texture than was already available, either in the United States or outside. He wrote later:

> I was confronted, amongst other problems, with the question what was to be done about windows since all window glass was of poor quality. I then perceived that the glass used for claret bottles and preserve jars was richer, finer and had a more beautiful quality in colour than any glass I could buy. I set to puzzling out this curious matter and found that the glass from which bottles are made contained the Oxides of Iron and other impurities which are left in the sand when that is melted.
>
> The problem of making the metallic oxides left in the 'impure' glass combine effectively took thirty years of experimenting with new firing furnaces and new methods of annealing glass.

Metallic oxides were added in small amounts to the clear-glass formula to make coloured glass, and great skill was required to judge the correct amount to obtain the exact tone wanted. Cobalt oxide in the form of cupric oxide coloured glass blue; iron oxide produced a green colour; manganese oxide produced a violet colour; gold, copper or selenium coloured glass red; coke, coal and other carbon oxides produced an amber colour; and black was produced from a combination of manganese, cobalt and iron.

While Tiffany was making his experiments at Heidt, using the earliest results in glass tiles for mantels and stained glass for windows, John La Farge, the artist and colourist, was also carrying out experiments at the same glasshouse. Although both were working at the same glasshouse at the same time, with similar aims, they became not partners but rivals, and rivalry increased over the years as they became fierce competitors for the same commissions. They were both founder members of the American School of Stained Glass.

Like Tiffany, La Farge applied for a patent for a coloured window glass, also in 1880, but earlier, in the February of that year. It seems that La Farge was persuaded by Tiffany to waive his patent and he forfeited its protection. Possibly he had been promised collaboration or partnership with Tiffany, but that never happened. Sometimes La Farge is credited with being the leader

RIGHT: Tiffany's landscape windows such as this one c.1900, replaced the mundane world outside with a magical world of glowing colour, light and shade.

At the American Red Cross Headquarters in Washington D.C. a large triple-panelled window was installed in 1918 with a design by Frederick Wilson. For the central panel Tiffany created a fantasy of medieval warfare in stained glass with the panels either side picturing the healing work of the Red Cross.

The enlargements of the Red Cross windows illustrate
clearly how Tiffany had achieved his aim — the entire
design is carried out by means of the colour in the glass
itself, the hands and faces of the figures, the folds of
draperies, the lights and shadows produced without using
paint or etching or enamelling of any kind.

and the originator, sometimes Tiffany. But it is clear that, backed by his family association and resources, Tiffany's subsequent success overwhelmed La Farge, and the resentment intensified.

One of the most important aims of Tiffany's experiments was to produce glass that would make it possible for the entire design of a window to be carried out by means of the colour in the glass itself. This meant that figures, their hands and faces, the folds of draperies, the shadows and lights on landscapes, must all be achieved without using any paint, etching or enamelling.

At the Heidt works a new glass was invented by Tiffany with great possibilities and promise. It was given the name drapery glass because the sheets of coloured glass were styled to represent folds in textiles, with three-dimensional effect. Workmen moved heavy corrugated rollers over the molten glass, punching and pressing and pulling it about with tongs until the right kind of drape was obtained in varying degrees of translucency for the fine folds of gowns or the voluminous folds of curtains.

"Bull's-eye" effects were produced by whirling the molten glass round on a rod. Solid lumps of glass were pressed into moulds while hot, giving a great number of facets; these could be set in windows like brilliant gems, changing colour at different angles and catching the light.

Tiles that were transparent, opaque, marbled and mottled with swirling streaks of colour or gleaming with an iridescent finish were produced. These were used as wall decorations and fireplace surrounds.

Tiffany used "bull's-eye" semicircular windows in the Church of the Sacred Heart, New York, in 1876. In effect, the design was like a series of preserve jar bottoms. In 1878 he designed a window with St Mark as the subject for the Episcopal Church in Islip, Long Island, using a series of tangential, circular pieces of glass surrounding the figure, outlined in the broadest way without "drawing" on the glass.

Opalescent glass was widely used by Tiffany and by La Farge in their windows and as time went on it became a special characteristic of American stained glass. Later critics have pointed out that by using opalescent glass Tiffany "was destroying as effectively as the seventeenth- and eighteenth-century glass enameller had done, the translucency of glass, which is the very soul of a medieval window".

Tiffany insisted always that his stained-glass windows were a purer expression of stained glass than those of medieval glass-makers because he could dispense with pigment. All the colour was in the glass and it was the way the light could be varied by the use of opalescent glass and gradations of tone colour that enabled him to create special effects. He was to prove this in his masterpieces. For the first time the glass itself was the sole means of denoting light and shade and perspective, by means of texture, changing colour and form. This was the exciting breakthrough.

Later Tiffany would be able to say: "By the aid of studies in chemistry and through years of experiments, I have found means to avoid the use of paints, etching or burning, or otherwise treating the surface of the glass so that now it is possible to produce figures in glass of which even the fleshtones are not superficially treated, built up of what I call 'genuine glass' because there are no tricks of the glassmaker needed to express flesh."

It has been said that this was perhaps the first time that "the medium was the message", but if that was so, then more variation was needed in the material, and experiments continued with iridescence, as that was one means of extending the colour range.

Tiffany was absorbed in glass experiments and possibilities, and he was also continuing to collect, amassing an array of artefacts. As well as antique glass he collected Oriental domestic ware, humble objects which showed good craftsmanship or illustrated particular techniques in their making. These functional and decorative objects in his collection included Chinese jade bowls, embroidered screens, ivory, jewellery, porcelain pots and jugs, Persian temple rugs, Islamic wall tiles and Egyptian beads. This was a new area of collecting at the time, as it was not classical art in the accepted sense. For example, he had a fine collection of Japanese swordguards, many of which had been acquired in 1868, when the emperor decreed that the Japanese army should carry firearms instead of swords, and the design of these objects served as source material for his own work.

He studied the techniques and design of everything he collected and absorbed understanding as if by osmosis. This was part of his lifelong quest for beauty and was also important to his belief that the best possible process of learning was by close association with beautiful objects, arts and crafts.

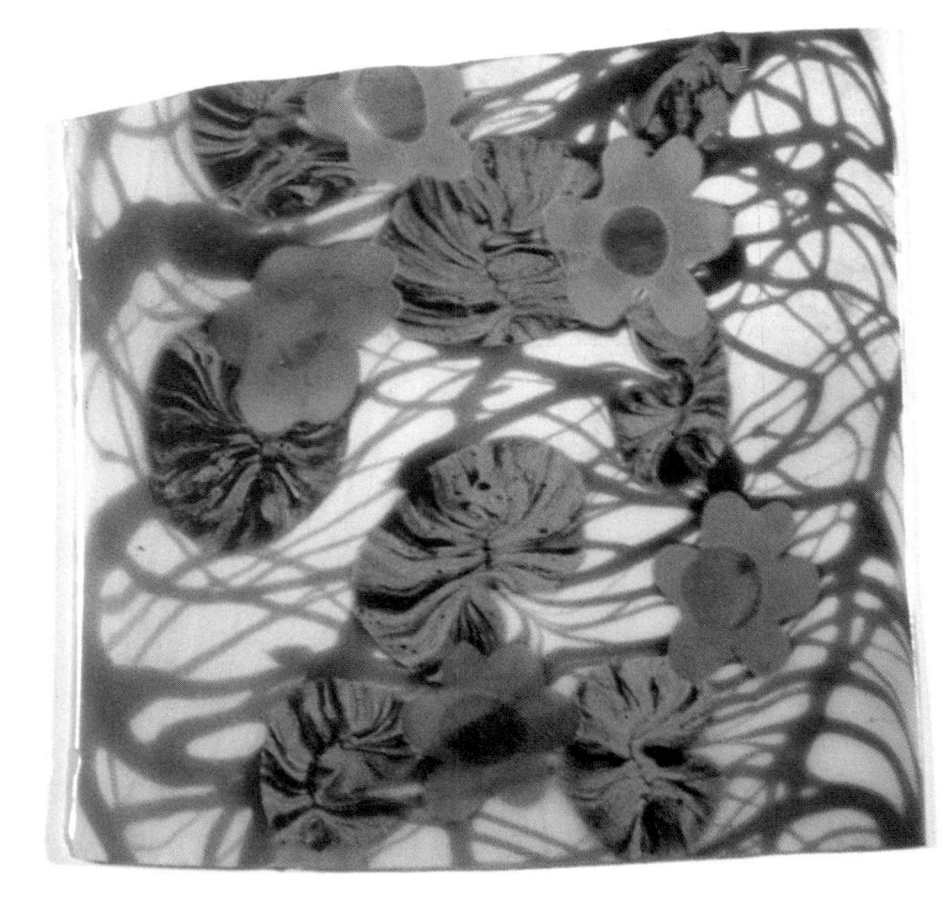

LEFT: **Lustre and agate tiles featured in many of Tiffany's interior designs. He used them in fireplace surrounds, incorporated them in table tops and in decorative freizes around windows and doors.**

He had been in Europe again in 1875, visiting the Paris Exposition, where Edward Moore won a Gold Medal and his father, Charles Tiffany, was made a Chevalier de la Legion d'Honneur. He travelled with his original mentor, Edward Moore, and was introduced to Samuel Bing, who imported Oriental items and supplied many of the unique objects in Moore's and Tiffany's collections. For Tiffany the meeting with Samuel Bing was the start of a long friendship and a very auspicious one. Some 20 years later Samuel Bing opened a shop in Paris which he called La Maison de l'Art Nouveau. This gave the Movement its focus and official title, and Bing was instrumental in introducing Tiffany's glasswork to Europe.

As Louis Tiffany became more and more absorbed in his experiments in glass, the team of Associated Artists began to drift apart. In 1883 it was decided to detach the artistic needlework side, controlled by Candace Wheeler, and she and her team expanded activities into textiles and wall-papers. "I think Mr Tiffany was rather glad to get rid of us all," she said, "for his wonderful experiments in glass iridescence ... meant far more to him at the time than association with other interests."

In the spring of the same year Tiffany took his first holiday in five years and went with his wife and children to St Augustine, Florida, in the hope that the trip would restore Mary to better health. She had been suffering from tuberculosis for 10 years. But despite the holiday and open-air treatment then prescribed for diseases of the chest, she died on 22 January, 1884.

They had been a devoted couple. Tiffany had always been able to share with Mary his hopes and dreams. He had absolute confidence in her and she was irreplaceable in his life. At the age of only 37 he became a widower with

RIGHT: **Tiffany's first experiments with coloured glass at Heidt Glasshouse developed from the pot-metal glass used for preserve jars and claret bottles. Plaques of rich glowing colour were first produced in the late 1870s and incorporated in decorative windows.**

three children, the eldest of whom was only 10.

His grief and disappointment extended from his home life to his work. He was in no mood to cater for the whims of difficult wealthy clients and turned for solace to the theatrical world, with two friends in particular, Steel MacKaye and Stanford White. It was for Steel MacKaye that Tiffany had worked on the curtain of the Madison Square Theater. Now MacKaye was contemplating opening a new theatre, which was to be called the Lyceum, and he was inspired by Oscar Wilde to build an ideal theatre "according to the highest standards of aesthetics and art". Wilde had praised Tiffany's work, saying: "From the same master hand which designed the curtain at the Madison Square Theater I would like very much to see a good decorative landscape in scene painting."

Tiffany was obviously the artist to undertake the Lyceum Theater decoration, though there had been some discussion between MacKaye and La Farge, Tiffany's great rival. Tiffany's offer to undertake the work for no fee, just a percentage of the profits, got him the job, and also intensified the competition between the two artists.

It was an exciting project, elevated to the highest level of artistic aims, and it had the advantage of the latest technical advances. It was the first theatre to be lit by electric light — Thomas A. Edison helped to install the footlights — and there were new folding seats. Everything in the design, it was said, was a departure from the hackneyed forms of theatrical decoration. "The electric light from the clustered globes pendant from the ceiling is soft and pleasantly diffused. Similar lights smoulder under green sconces along the face of the gallery, like fire in monster emeralds ... But these things are not

obtrusive. A master hand has blent them into a general effect, avoiding all aggressive detail."

The success of the theatre design was not matched by that of its first production *Dakolar*, which ran for only two months. Not only were there no profits for Tiffany but there was not even enough money to pay the bills. Tiffany was forced to sue and ended up owning the theatre until a new manager was able to put it on a paying basis. In the process he lost money heavily, his excursion into the theatrical world costing him the profits of all his years of hard work in interior design.

It was a sad time for Tiffany. The collapse of his interior decorating career with Associated Artists and the financial disaster of the Lyceum Theater, all following so closely on the death of Mary, were hard to take. Charles Tiffany became greatly concerned about his son's involvement with high-flown theatrical ventures, chorus girls and other fast company. He felt the way for Louis to restore himself was to become absorbed again in the artistic work for which he had so much talent. He announced that he would build a Tiffany family house and Louis would be in full charge of its decoration.

The Tiffany house was built on Madison Avenue, once known as "The Avenue of the Gods" because of the number of churches along its length. It was huge, vast — some said the most beautiful modern domestic building ever seen — with a massive arched entrance, a grill and porte-cochère, an elevator, balconies and loggias.

On the top floors Louis Tiffany designed a studio and apartment for himself and his children and in decorating the studio he produced the first example of American Art Nouveau.

The studio appears from photographs and contemporary reports to have been a glorious, eclectic, decorative jungle, richly Indian, with lamps on chains and plants of many lands. It was dominated by a curving free-form central fireplace which reached upward in a single column towards the roof like "the bole of a great tree". The fireplace was open on four sides so that blazing logs would illuminate the iridescent lamps and bright vases and beautiful things everywhere about it. It is described in *The Art Work of Louis C. Tiffany* as having "colored tiles and the cinnabar red so much loved by the Japanese, iridescent glass and shelves full of ceramics in subdued tones meet the eye in

RIGHT: Charles Tiffany commissioned a grand New York residence for his family with design by Louis Tiffany. In designing the studio and apartment on the top floors for himself and his family Louis Tiffany created the first example of American Art Nouveau.

every direction". Others have said it had a magical quality, something of an Arabian Nights dream in New York.

Tiffany continued to occupy the top floor studio and the connecting apartment as his town residence until the day of his death. Here for many decades he lavishly entertained friends, here his three children grew up. He married again in 1886, to Louise Wakeford Knox, the daughter of a Presbyterian minister. The Tiffany family approved his choice, glad that his family life and his working life were now restored. Charles Tiffany's commissioning of the apartment block for his sons and daughters had compensated for past disappointments and Louis could strike forth boldly again.

He was experienced and talented, original, well versed in the arts of America, Europe and the East. He had found the financial disaster of the Lyceum Theater a chastening experience and now accepted not only his father's help and advice but also his kind of professionalism. In 1885 he relaunched his business as the Tiffany Glass Company. Set up in a more businesslike way, it catered for professionals rather than private clients, and the glass which later made his name and international fame occupied his attention full-time. He took on the role of creative director and master designer, employed specialist craftsmen and concentrated on his work with a new maturity and renewed vigour.

From this point Tiffany's career began to move ahead strongly into a new phase of success as leading architects gave the Tiffany Glass Company orders for stained-glass windows for homes, churches and institutions. Tiffany began to obtain the kind of glass he needed to carry out his designs, experimenting all the time to "make a material in which colors and combinations of colors, hues, shades, tints and tones should be there without surface treatment as far as possible".

Again he was extraordinarily lucky in his timing. As the rich interiors of his work with Associated Artists' had come at just the right time, with the prosperous American industrial barons wanting to show off their wealth in magnificent houses, so his breakthrough in coloured glass for windows coincided with the great religious fervour that was sweeping America. All over the country more and more churches were being built in the new towns growing up along the railroads which crossed from the east coast to the west.

In every church stained-glass windows were in demand, to give these new buildings a sense of substance and importance. Leading citizens and clergymen were honoured with specially commissioned stained-glass windows and dear ones were remembered with window memorials. Tiffany inspired the fashion, and it was Tiffany windows that were wanted.

He had set himself to rediscover the brilliance of the medieval stained glass that filled the great bays of gothic aisles and chancels with splendour. He had deplored the coldness of later windows, particularly in northern Europe, where cloudy skies and the dark atmosphere of cities combined with the dim colours in the glass to depress the spirit instead of uplifting it with heavenly visions. "Our climate invites to sumptuous colors," he said. He believed that American skies and atmosphere "seem to ask for interiors sheltering the eyes from an excess brilliancy".

But he found that he had to contend with the tradition in the Episcopal Church of the United States that still looked reverentially towards the Church of England, whence it sprang. "The prejudices of clergymen and vestrymen are in favor of British glass for windows," Tiffany said, "notwithstanding its coldness and lack of character." His colours were considered gaudy, altogether too bright, by some churchmen.

As a colourist, he expressed his own boldness of vision and character in colour. He deplored the timidity of neutral tints in sculpture, architecture, pottery and textiles, putting it down to lack of courage and "the obscure feeling that color is danger". He felt that the public must be educated to distinguish between deep, strong colouration and gaudiness.

His methods of designing stained-glass windows demanded much care and constant attention. The artist had to superintend every stage of the work, not just sketch an outline and hand the work over to a foreman.

> As in painting the introduction of new color in one part of the canvas or tint or tone, has its blissful or baneful effect upon all that has gone before, so with a stained glass window, no other eyes than those of the original artist can tell whether the fresh note added to the rest is the right one or wrong one. Infinite, endless labor makes the masterpiece.

Tiffany was greatly in demand for his pictorial windows, but many critics believed he was at his best in abstract designs. Robert W. de Forest, one of the first to own a Tiffany-designed window, recalled the chief design as "the use of translucent quartz pebbles, which he and I picked up together on the beach at Montauk".

John Ruskin preferred random designs and pebble clusters to the fashionable figure windows, rejoicing "in a glowing mosaic of bright colour; for that is what the glass has the special gift and right of producing". Other critics admired Tiffany's marvellous mastery of technique, but not his designs.

It was only gradually that Tiffany began to depart from the figure windows, taking a step similar to the post-Impressionist painters in breaking up form and setting areas of colour one against the other.

John Gilbert Lloyds said that Tiffany's windows were characterized "by brilliantly colored scenes, highly realistic, artistic designs and almost a fruity use of shape and color. Constantly striving to improve his glass coloring for faces and drapery, which in Europe were painted or enamelled on, he gave more life to stained glass than it had in age. Although stylized and dated, Tiffany windows established a precedent and affected the public taste and preference for decades to come."

It was his pictorial work that made Tiffany so fashionable in America. His stained-glass windows were commissioned by architects and could be seen in prestigious institutions such as the Smithsonian and Yale University. He was also responsible for ornamental windows and panels on the ferry boats that plied the Hudson River between New Jersey and Manhattan. In every state and town, everyone wanted Tiffany glass. The new class of industrial magnates commissioned him: in Pittsburgh, Andrew Carnegie; in New York, Henry Osborne Havemeyer and Arthur Heckscher. There were memorials to presidents and magnates. Five windows were commissioned by the Temple of the Latter Day Saints in Salt Lake City (which could be viewed only by Mormons). One of Tiffany's most important patrons was the entrepreneur Joseph Raphael Delemar, rich from gold and lead-ore mining and business ventures in the colonies. He commissioned five Tiffany windows, including *The Bathers,* a fine pair of bird panels, and spherical Tiffany butterfly lampshades for his subterranean swimming-pool illumination.

Tiffany windows were expensive. Alastair Duncan, in his authoritative book *Tiffany Windows*, quotes as an example the Apocalypse Simpson Memorial, installed in the Calvary Methodist Church in Alleghenys at a cost of $3,500 at a time when stained-glass artisans were paid $3 a day and their supervisors $21 a week. St Paul Preaching to the Athenians Memorial in the Lafayette Avenue Presbyterian Church in Brooklyn cost $5,000. Tiffany, it is said, lost more commissions because of high prices than for any other reason.

Noting how Tiffany windows, commercially successful and conventional in design, were flooding the country, some artists began to say that Tiffany had sold out to commerce. But Tiffany claimed that he was the first American artist to design for the industrial age, breaking free of classic formulas, working to no fundamental rules. He believed that his new, reorganized business would be unique, he would produce pictures in glass more lasting and beautiful than any rendered in paint. Each work would be unique, with freshness and individuality. He would expand wider and wider, with new and daring projects, and provide a vast audience with visual excitement. He had a vision of an art industry, a museum without walls.

His studio and apartment, which so expressed his ideals, became an atelier where he hoped to educate many young talented people, as he himself had been educated by exposure to beautiful objects. He saw himself as the master, encouraging the talent of others, like della Robbia or Rubens. The same system was later to be adopted by Frank Lloyd Wright and the German Bauhaus under Walter Gropius and others.

With his aims so clear and his success so great in America, it must have been a shock for Tiffany, on a visit to Paris in 1889 for the Exposition Universelle, to find that a window by his rival John La Farge was winning all the attention and praise for its unique colour and technique. Tiffany had to prove that he could produce much better examples of such windows and achieve international recognition.

Edward C. Moore was also in Paris, to receive five Gold Medals, the Grand Prix for Tiffany & Co and the Chevalier de la Legion d'Honneur. So, through him, Tiffany made a point of renewing his acquaintance with Samuel Bing, from whom he had bought so many Oriental treasures for his collection. He arranged with Samuel Bing that he would make windows for display.

Samuel Bing's shop attracted artists interested in new materials and techniques. Van Gogh often visited it in the eighties, browsing through the Japanese prints. It was becoming a meeting place for a group of artists calling themselves Nabis, who, like Tiffany, were putting colour before form and were fascinated by the separation of colour into pure, flat planes in medieval stained-glass windows.

Samuel Bing welcomed Tiffany and their reunion was the challenge and impetus Tiffany's work needed at that point. Their association was a long and advantageous one and it began with a window, *The Four Seasons*, exhibited in Paris in 1892 and later in London. It was a "domestic" window, its descriptive panels of the four seasons enclosed by an ornamental border. The four abstract paintings of the seasons symbolically evoked the times of year with colourful vegetation and landscape and were edged by free-flowing decorative borders with jewel-like insets of coloured glass. Summer is perhaps the most evocative, overhung with leafy shapes, with heavy-leaded outlines of leaves and full-blown roses, a distant lake and purple mountains beyond. Changing colour in the glass itself forms the perspective, and there is no etching on the material.

With *The Four Seasons* Tiffany achieved the aims he had been working towards for a decade and amazed the critics who had been denigrating his popular pictorial work in stained glass. Tiffany naturally took great pleasure in their praise.

As a result of this association with Samuel Bing a link was established between Tiffany and the French painters who seemed to be working on the same lines. Ten windows of Tiffany glass with designs by French artists chosen by Bing were commissioned: Paul Ranson designed two; Pierre Bonnard, Eugene Grasset, Henri Ibels, Ker-Xavier Roussel, Paul Serusier, Henri de Toulouse-Lautrec, Edouard Vuillard and Felix Valloton each designed one. Three years, later when the 10 windows went on display, Tiffany prepared a brochure for Bing, proudly proclaiming that American stained glass was supreme and in particular that Tiffany glass was superior to medieval. One French critic described this statement as *"bizarre manifeste"*. But for Tiffany the association with Bing helped him to work boldly, to seek new means of expression and to take his place on the international scene.

RIGHT: "Summer" — a panel of Louis Tiffany's *Four Seasons* window exhibited in Paris in 1892. With this masterly evocative work in stained glass Tiffany amazed his critics and established his place on the international art scene.

Samuel Bing also made a survey of American art and architecture for the French government and he was entertained by Tiffany on his visit. The exchange of ideas encouraged both of them to increase their efforts to promote a new kind of art, to make available to a wider public objects that were both useful and beautiful, objects that could be produced for the many, not just the few. They were both businessmen and respected each other's business sense as well as artistic aims; they were both sure of their values and their ability to discriminate. From their discussions they developed greater confidence in themselves as educators of public taste and Tiffany's conviction that he was a genius grew.

They both agreed with William Morris on the importance of keeping handicrafts alive, but where Morris's handmade objects were too expensive for the general public, Tiffany believed that materials made by machine could achieve beauty in the home for the masses.

It was Bing who inspired Tiffany to design a chapel for the World's Columbian Exhibition in Chicago in 1893. His exhibit, consisting of a chapel, a light room and a dark room, was not ready for the opening of the fair but was shown in New York and later shipped to Chicago, where it became the sensation of the exhibition.

The chapel was opulent and vibrant with luminous colour. The altar was white, with a white and iridescent glass mosaic front. Behind it the reredos was composed of a pictorial, iridescent glass mosaic of peacocks and vine scrolls, set into black marble. The mosaic was the focal point and surmounting it was a series of concentric Romanesque round arches, decorated with relief interlaces overlaid in gold. These arches were supported by clusters of columns with carved capitals, the shafts covered with glass mosaic of reds, greens and browns in random patterns, set with pearls and semiprecious stones. Light was admitted by a series of 12 stained-glass windows and an elaborate cruciform bejewelled sanctuary lamp was suspended in the centre of the dome-like space. A million pieces of glass went into its making.

It was said that entering the chapel may well have been an experience similar to that had by the people of Ravenna when their own Byzantine mosaics were new. Flanking the chapel were the dark room in blue-green and the light room in silver and pearl, lit by a chandelier of mother of pearl.

ABOVE: **At the World's Columbian Exposition in Chicago in 1893 Americans were proud to see the progress their country had made in arts and crafts. They criticized foreign exhibits as too refined and acclaimed the sumptuous opulence of Tiffany's Byzantine chapel with its peacock reredos of iridescent glass mosaics, marble with scroll borders and gorgeous hanging lamps.**

Tiffany's chapel was undeniably effective. It became a symbol of American design because it was considered to equal anything produced abroad. A wealthy Chicago widow, Celia Whipple Wallace, arranged for it to be donated to the Cathedral of St John the Divine in New York, where it was installed in the crypt and used for services until 1911.

For some people the sumptuous wealth of Tiffany Byzantine, with its mosaic, scroll borders, gorgeous hanging lamps and marble inlays, was altogether too much. It was considered too heavy, somewhat cloying and oversweet. To European eyes much of Tiffany's work was puzzling in its eclecticism. While there was much that was original, full of quality and merit, with an almost mystical fervour in the sumptuous colour and belief in the beauty of the materials used, the elements did not seem to fuse into a style.

The problem would seem to be that Americans were at this time looking for a truly American style, a trend in taste, in colour, in line and proportion, that would go to form a national style. Cecilia Waern made this point in *The Studio* in 1897, pointing out that with America still in a stage of assimilation, "Perhaps it is one of the real achievements of L. C. Tiffany that he has caught this, given it a voice. A Tiffany room is a thing apart, with an unmistakeable American note — in spite of its eclecticism."

# MANY
# SPENDORED
# GLASS

"Tiffany glass, with its swirling patterns, its strange iridescent colors, its marbled designs, its curious free-form shapes, its clear, brilliant patternings trapped as if by magic in the texture of the object, was without a doubt the most beautiful glass produced in its time."

MARIO AMAYA

THE PARIS EXPOSITION OF 1889 had far-reaching effects on Tiffany. He saw there for the first time glass vases being made by Emile Gallé of Nancy. Enamelled, engraved and tinted they were creating a sensation, for their technical brilliance and artistic merit.

Louis Tiffany and Emile Gallé were contemporaries and there were many resemblances between the two men. Gallé was born in 1846, two years before Tiffany. His father ran a successful decorative glassware and faience business, which he took over and built up from a small local concern to perhaps the largest luxury glassware factory in Europe.

All through his career, Gallé conducted experiments and produced creations that were acclaimed. He wrote extensively about the theories that lay behind his work. He had realized that decorative glass had great scope, that glass was an infinitely variable medium. Where the Venetians and the great glass-makers had been striving for crystal-clear glass and achieving brilliant effects with etching and engraving, he was producing with remarkable success coloured glass with the variations and intensity of precious stones.

Gallé was an artist and an entrepreneur, talented in both spheres, but like Tiffany, when he was forced to combine them, it was not always with complete success. Like Tiffany also, Gallé drew inspiration from nature for form and decoration, and felt the urge to achieve something new in art. Both succeeded and reached the high point in their respective careers at the time of the triumph of Art Nouveau at the 1900 Paris Exposition.

Gallé's cameo glass was already being highly praised at the 1889 exhibition and this ensured the commercial success of his Nancy factory. It made a deep impression on Tiffany and he returned to America inspired with new challenges and fresh determination.

Other Europeans were experimenting with glass: crackled glass by Leveille; hardstone effects were being achieved by Loetz; early iridescent glass vessels were being produced by Lobmeyer, Pantin and Webb; and formal cameo-carved vessels were being produced by various English Stourbridge firms.

Arthur J. Nash, trained at Stourbridge, Worcestershire, was manager of one of the Webb glassworks. He was touring the United States in 1892 to promote his firm's wares when Tiffany persuaded him to join in the founding of a new glassworks and factory at Corona, Long Island.

RIGHT: Peacock Lamp with bronze base — the technique of making lamps was on the same principle as the stained-glass windows. The pieces of glass were cut to the artist's design and the leading was woven around the glass.

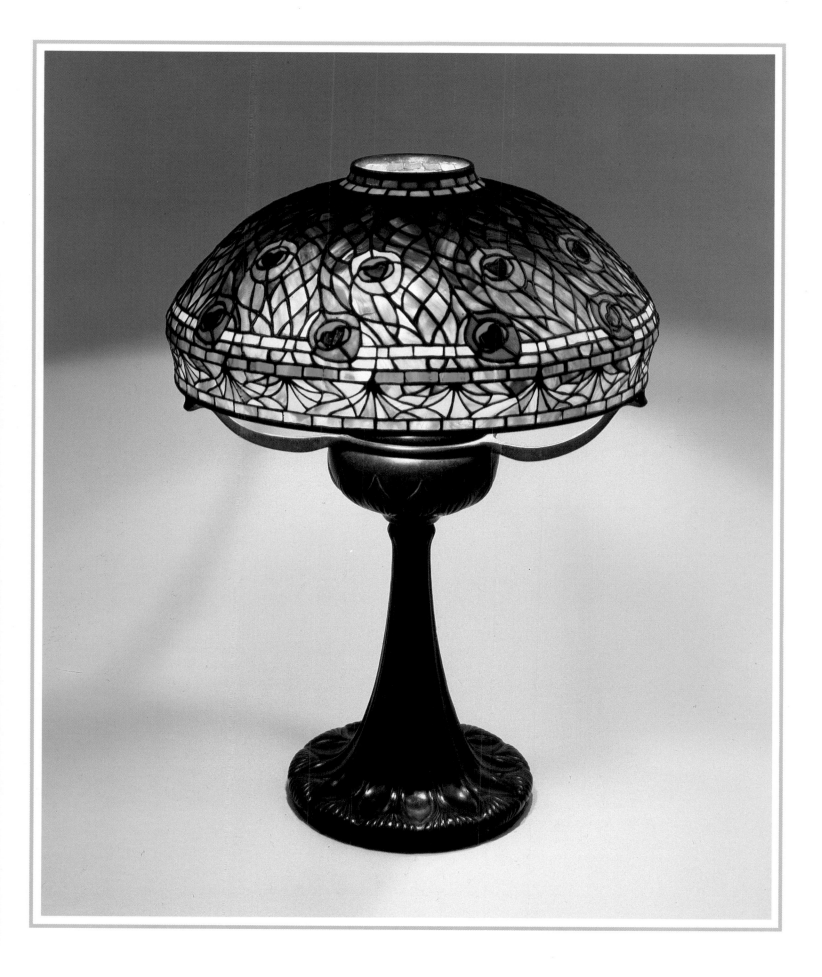

Tiffany had found that to get the glass he wanted it was essential to have his own glassworks, to control chemical experiments and glass production, and he employed Arthur Nash as chief designer and manager. Nash was a technical expert, familiar with traditional methods and modern English glass-making techniques and it seems certain that Tiffany could not have achieved his dramatic success without him.

Soon after it opened the Corona factory burned down, as two of Tiffany's previous glassworks had done. Undaunted by arson, Tiffany rebuilt and Nash remained. The firm quickly expanded, with more glass-workers recruited from England and a special works within the factory built to produce blown-glass objects.

Nash stayed with Tiffany for 15 years, bringing his sons into the business, and they later claimed that their father had not been given due credit for his part in Tiffany's success. Certainly to Nash should go much of the praise for the superior quality of Tiffany blown glass that was maintained through the years. It is thought most likely that Nash — known as "a wizard with the blow pipe" — produced the earliest flower-form vases in free-flowing shapes.

The success of the Tiffany Glass and Decorating Company, and the beauty Tiffany blown glass achieved, came about because Nash headed a team of highly skilled craftsmen, Tiffany provided the direction, purpose and inspiration, and he and his father, Charles Tiffany, financed the operation. It took years of work and thousands of dollars, but Tiffany admitted no technical or financial limits to his creativity.

In 1894 Tiffany registered Favrile as a trademark — "a name easily spoken and readily recalled," he said. The name derived from the Old English fabrile, meaning handmade or belonging to a craftsman.

Favrile glass, as Tiffany describes it in his dictated autobiography, "is distinguished by certain remarkable shapes and brilliant or deeply toned colors, usually iridescent like the wings of certain American butterflies, the necks of pigeons and peacocks, the wing-covers of various beetles". In the original application it was described more prosaically as "a composition of various coloured glasses, worked together while hot".

The earliest recorded glass was Egyptian. Glasswork of an advanced kind in Egypt is dated around 1450 BC. Then, coloured glass was achieved with softened canes or rods of glass wound round a core into the shape of a vase. The mass, which

RIGHT: **When the first Favrile art glass was produced in 1894 Tiffany sent examples to Samuel Bing in Paris who was immediately amazed and delighted by it.**

then had the consistency of treacle, was reheated to fuse the canes of coloured glass together to produce wavy patterns. Glass-blowing was devised in Syria in the 1st century BC, at first simply by blowing into moulds, then with a hollow pipe which achieved much thinner glass. Roman glass was an offshoot of Syrian and Alexandrian work and factories were established for mass quantity production. In Imperial Rome glass was used as decoration in bathrooms, for wall tiles and mosaics, as well as vessels.

It was this sort of glass, unearthed by the archaeologists, that had inspired Tiffany with its soft iridescence and that he was now trying to emulate — just as modern painters, he said, have tried to rival in painting the tones affected by age on old paintings. It called for chemical knowledge and great perseverance.

Tiffany's team at the Corona glassworks was soon producing an extraordinary range of lustred effects, and much of the first successful glass-blowing production was sent to Bing in Paris, who was amazed and delighted by it. He said: "After all the accomplishments of the Venetians, of Gallé and others, it was still possible to innovate, to utilize glass in a new way that was so often opaque and matte, with a

surface that was like skin to the touch, silky and delicate."

Bing described the method as follows:

> Look at the incandescent ball of glass as it comes out of the furnace;
> it is slightly dilated by the initial inspiration of air. The workman
> charges it at certain pre-arranged points with small quantities of
> glass of different textures and different colours and in the operation
> is hidden the germ of the intended ornamentation. The little ball is
> then returned to the fire to be heated. Again it is subjected to a
> similar treatment (the process sometimes being repeated as many as
> twenty times) and, when all the different glasses have been
> combined and manipulated in different ways, and the article has
> been brought to its definite state as to form and dimensions, it
> presents this appearance: the motifs introduced into the ball when it
> was small have grown with the vase itself, but in differing
> proportions; they have lengthened and broadened, while each tiny
> ornament fills the place assigned to it in advance in the mind of
> the artist.

In this way all kinds of ornamental ideas could be fused into the glass: flowers floated within it magically — morning glories, roses, tiny daisies, trailing vine leaves and stems. In some showpiece Favrile bowls miraculous effects were produced: goldfish floating amid seaweed and clear water, all in the glass itself.

The most complex were the vases in what is described as paperweight glass, so technically difficult to produce that they baffle modern glass-makers today. Sometimes coloured abstractions were produced in the glass that it was impossible to repeat and these became known as accidentals. These are among the most rare of Tiffany vases because they were so difficult and costly to make.

The millefiori technique, in which little petals, flowers or leaves were annealed all about with clear glass until a vase was formed in which the flowers hung suspended, was first developed by the Venetians in the 2nd century BC. Thin rods of coloured glass were arranged in groups so that five white rods grouped round a yellow rod could be cut to appear as a daisy.

Superb examples of
Tiffany's art on display at
the Haworth Art Gallery,
Accrington, Lancashire.
(ABOVE) Vases of elegant
flower form shape,
shimmering gold finish
and trailing decoration of
leaves. (RIGHT) A virtuoso
showpiece with lifelike
goldfish swimming
through the waterweed.

LEFT: An Agate vase (centre) made c.1910 with two marblized vases, the glass imitating the striations and veinings found in natural agate and marble.

RIGHT: An iridescent blue Egyptian onion-flower form vase (centre) with two blue millefiori vases. This beautiful iridescent blue was less popular than gold originally so less was produced. Now it is so rare it has become much sought after and costly.

Supreme examples of Tiffany millefiori vases are the range of morning glory designs. Many of these were produced later, into the 20th century, as the technique was developed. Reactive paperweight glass was another variation, using an inner layer of reactive glass which changed colour when heated.

Agate wares were produced that imitated stones such as chalcedony, jasper, agate and marble. These effects were achieved by putting a number of variously coloured opaque glasses into the same melting pot and heating them together.

Tiffany had filed a patent for lustreware back in 1880, describing it as "a highly-iridescent one and of pleasing metallic lustre changeable from one to the other, depending upon the direction of the visual ray and the brilliancy or dullness of the light falling upon or passing through the glass".

Lustre glass was made by dissolving salts of rare metals in the molten glass and keeping them in an oxidized state while subjecting the glass to the flame to produce the chemical reaction. Then the piece was sprayed with chloride, which made it crackle and break up into a mass of fine lines that

picked up the light. Different effects were produced with different metals —
pearly sheen, golden lustre, rich deep blues.

Gold lustre, it was said, was formed from $20 gold pieces, and gold was
also used to achieve the much sought-after red pieces.

As Tiffany's earliest experimental shapes were based closely on Roman
vases and Islamic shapes, it was difficult to tell them from the originals now
that he had the technique of giving them the golden lustre of buried glass.

He did not claim to have invented iridescent glass, but Tiffany's iridescent
glass had a soft, incandescent sheen unlike the hard mirror-like surface of
that produced by Lobmeyer and others. Naturally he had the problem that
many copied him — "the mark of honor which is called the sincerest flattering". But it was said the colours were thin and flat when compared with
Tiffany pieces.

Peacock feather patterns were produced in iridescent glass. It was probably Arthur Nash who invented the peacock iridescent markings on glass
vases and plates, a direct inspiration from Whistler's Peacock Room in
London. Peacocks were a recurring motif of the Art Nouveau movement.
Bing wrote a rapturous description of a peacock feather vase in a later exhibition of Tiffany ware at the Grafton Galleries in London: "Just as in the natural
feather itself, we find here a suggestion of the impalpable, the tenuity of the
fronds and their pliability ... Never, perhaps has any man carried to greater
perfection the art of faithfully rendering Nature in her most seductive
aspects." He marvelled at the technical achievement of "assigning in advance
to each morsel of glass, whatever its color or chemical composition, the exact
place which it is to occupy when the article leaves the glassblower's hands —
this truly unique art is combined in these peacock's feathers with the charm
of iridescence which bathes the subtle and velvety ornamentation with an
almost supernatural light."

Jack-in-the-pulpit vases were also made in iridescent gold or blue glass,
taking their name from the flower of the convolvulus. It was one of several
examples of Tiffany taking a humble hedgerow flower and giving it an
amazing sophistication in iridescent glass — and making it, in the process,
extremely popular. These vases are spectacularly shaped, with single delicate
flowers poised on a slender stem.

RIGHT TOP: **A punch bowl
of iridescent gold made
from non-lead glass.**

BOTTOM: **Iridescent gold
vases with Egyptian
inspired decoration c.1910.**

LEFT: Example of Tiffany's daring originality, experimenting in the potential of glass with haphazard patterns of rough textures and exciting contrasts of surfaces. Basalt or talc was then added and the surface was gold lustred.

RIGHT TOP: Lava glass vase 1909. Molten glass spilt over a rough surface produced the volcanic effect.

Basalt or talc was added to the molten glass to form Lava vases. They simulated the effects of volcanic forces on glass, in a free-form kind of expressionism representing the violence of nature, in black and rough textures.

In Cypriote glass Tiffany set out to recapture the appearance of antique glass with finely pitted, nacreous surfaces, corroded and decayed by time, irregular and abstract patterned. This was done by rolling the glass in pulverized crumbs and then lustring the encrusted surface.

Cameo glass was produced and some particularly beautiful effects were achieved in water lily vases overlaid in low relief. The basis for cameo carving is a vessel of two differently coloured glasses, sometimes with a layer between. A translucent yellow could be overlaid with red glass on which the outer layer was cut, carved and ground away to leave the design in relief on the background. The Portland Vase in the British Museum, thought to be of first-century AD Roman origin, is the most famous example of cameo glass. Tiffany, like Gallé — leader of the vogue in France — was inclined to use rather sickly combinations of colours at times.

Although the first Favrile art glass was produced at the Corona factory in 1894, Tiffany did not launch his new product on the market for another two years. He first sent glass to Samuel Bing and then sent examples to museums and art galleries in Europe, America and the Far East.

Items were sent to the Smithsonian Institution in Washington, to the Musée des Arts Décoratifs in Paris and to the Imperial Museum of Fine Arts in Tokyo and a collection was donated to the Metropolitan Museum of Art in New York by Henry Havemeyer. The Art Institute of Chicago, the Victoria and Albert Museum in London, the Royal Museum in Berlin, the Cincinnati Museum of Art and the Boston Museum of Fine Arts also received Favrile-glass presentations.

Some museums later denied that they received their collections during this period, but it is clear that Tiffany used this method of introducing his art glass to a worldwide discerning audience. It was inspired publicity for the commercial launch of his bowls and vases and ensured an immediate favourable reception.

Joseph Briggs, another Englishman, joined Tiffany in 1890, following a three-month visit to New York when he was 17. His rise to the top of the

RIGHT: Jack-in-the-pulpit vase — one of Tiffany's most successful Art Nouveau designs the slenderness of the stem accentuates the wide open spread of curly corolla in glistening glass.

ABOVE: **Three Cameo Vases** — carving to create a cameo effect, the outer layer cut away to leave a design in relief on the inner layer, originated in ancient Egypt. It was developed in England and in France, notably by Gallé. Tiffany produced some fine lustred cameo vases.

LEFT: A Favrile paperweight vase and a Cypriote vase. With Cypriote glass Tiffany set out to produce the appearance of ancient glass that had been buried for centuries, the surfaces corroded, pitted and nacreous, the colour and pattern haphazard.

RIGHT TOP: The celebrated Cameo Vases of Emile Gallé — introduced at the Paris Exhibition of 1889. Gallés superb technique and realization of the possibilities of decorative glass greatly impressed and influenced Tiffany.

RIGHT BELOW: Two intaglio vases by Tiffany (left). Intaglio is the reverse of cameo, the design cut away from the outer layer of glass leaving the pattern in one colour in relief, Cypriote iridescent vase (centre) and a green table centre piece (right).

LEFT: A miniature lamp by Emile Gallé of double overlay glass and bronze. Gallé's best work showed his technical brilliance combined with an emotional response to nature, a love of symbolism, a hint of the decadent and the bizarre that made Art Nouveau so mysterious and extraordinary.

organization was swift, and he became Tiffany's personal assistant, making a particular study of mosaic work. By 1902 he was manager of the Mosaic Department, in charge of some of the most spectacular work produced . He ran the furnaces until they closed in 1928, working for Tiffany for 40 years, until his death. He never returned to England, but he sent a quantity of Tiffany glass to his family in Accrington, Lancashire. This collection, later donated by the Briggs family to the Haworth Art Gallery in Accrington, is now the finest single collection of Tiffany glass in Europe.

While Tiffany was developing Favrile glass and experimenting with all kinds of coloured glass, much pot-metal glass of glorious colour was produced which could never find a place in the stained-glass windows. Stores of it accumulated. Glass was stacked away at Tiffany's inner sanctum, half-studio, half-workshop.

Cecilia Waern has described in an article in *The Studio* in 1897, how "choice pieces of blown glass lie around, awaiting attention from Mr Tiffany ... odds and ends of all kinds ... bits of unused metal work and other representatives of suggestive experiments, new departures or frank failures ... The back stairs and premises are full of waifs and strays of abandoned essays in every direction." Tiffany himself said: "It was evident that an industry pushed so far ought to strive to lower the annual deficit by the utilization of by-products, just like any other."

This was the sound commercial reason for turning to small glass — and to lamps in particular — thus making use of the glass left over from stained-glass windows, adapting the same technique with leading. But whereas in stained glass Tiffany had to contend against the tradition in favour of British glass and a certain timidity about the reaction to his bright colours, the success of his small glass and his lamps was immediate. They appealed to everybody, there was universal approval of their decorative charm, of the leaded shades that gave a pleasing diffused quality to the light.

All Tiffany's favourite nature themes appear in lamps: peacocks and dragonflies, trees in blossom, trailing flowers and brilliant blooms. The shades were worked with detailed juxtaposition of glass: the stems like trunks of trees and stems of flowers, the bases like roots, or like lily pads, each combining with the other to make a satisfying whole.

Glass had long been employed to protect the flickering flames of oil lamps and gas. Now, with the coming of electricity, the light was stronger, harder, not so flattering and romantic. Tiffany lamps came at the right moment to cast a magic glow over the new harsh modern light that was so efficient and yet so unromantic. Once again, Louis Tiffany was lucky with his timing.

There were floor lamps, ceiling lamps, table lamps, chandeliers, filigree lamps, spider's webs and purple globes, trellis lamps on which grapes or clematis trailed. One of the most popular was the wistaria lamp, offered in the original catalogue as item No. 342 at a price of $350. Today this spectacular lamp is a highly prized collector's item and its price in the saleroom has increased at least a hundredfold.

Many of these lamps in floral designs, hydrangeas and poinsettias, Oriental poppies and flowering lotus and cherry, were the design work of the team Tiffany had gathered about him. Whereas the Favrile vases and bowls were individually crafted, each a unique expression of Tiffany's artistic ideals, the lamps which first appeared in 1895 were so popular and the demand so great that he had to find some means of mass production. He set up an assembly line at the Corona works to put the lamps together. A prototype of a leaded shade with the glass pieces cut to the artist's design and the leading woven around the glass was on the same principle as the stained-glass window or the mosaic.

When he first started his workshops he found that the only way to get his ideas carried out was to train the workmen himself, then give each of the workmen apprentices to train. At one point the men went on strike, the only strike in any Tiffany firm, because they had too many apprentices. Tiffany's answer was to let them all go, replacing them with girls from the art schools, where they had some training in using their eyes and their hands and could develop with his training.

"At present", wrote Cecilia Waern in *The Studio* in 1897, "there are forty or fifty young women employed in the glass workshop, working at either mosaic or windows, generally ornamental. The larger memorial windows are, as a rule, put together by men (in other workshops). The work of both men and women is directed by the ubiquitous chief."

RIGHT: The grape table lamp was designed by Mrs Curtis Freschel at Tiffany Studios. The lamps that have become the most prized are those with an irregular lower border to the shade, formed here by the clusters of purple grapes hanging below the leaves.

LEFT: Iridescent glass lamp with base of bronze and reticulated jade green glass. Reticulated glass is now a very rare form of Tiffany art glass.

TOP: Lamps with a shade border of poinsettias (left) and lemon leaves (right).

LEFT: Lamp with an opalescent shade giving a pearly softness to the light.

Hundreds, sometimes thousands of each lamp design were made and sold. As with the vases, imitators were many, but none matched Tiffany for quality. Tiffany's team produced a constant flow of ideas, and while his creative energy provided the drive, his individual artists were allowed scope to choose colours and textures. The range of colours to choose from by the end of the century was truly amazing — as many as 5,000 colours and varieties — and in this way each lamp, although mass produced, was still individual and unique.

Some of the outstanding lamp designs were by women, encouraged to develop their talents by Tiffany at a time when the suffragette movement had scarcely been heard of. The wistaria lamp with its random-edged shade and multicoloured tesserae intricately leaded, was the work of Mrs Curtis Freschel and it won an award in 1902 at the International Exhibition of Modern Decorative Arts in Turin.

Mrs Clara Driscoll was responsible for the elegant dragonfly lampshade which won a prize at the Paris International Exposition in 1900. It is a lovely, imaginative piece of work; the insects, with their wings spread, hang head-downwards round the dome of the shade forming a fringe effect. Each wing is made up of minute fragments of coloured glass, set in delicate leading and the dome of the lamp, randomly decorated with raindrops, is set with semiprecious stones, all on a bronze, twisted vine base.

Tiffany was paying particular attention as time went on to the base of lamps, realizing the scope they offered for work of artistic design. He opened a foundry and metal shop at the Corona factory in 1897 so that bronze and copper could be made on the premises. He designed the famous lilypad lamps in bronze, with slender clusters of flower shapes springing on slender bronze stems from a lilypad base, and it won a Grand Prize at the Turin Exhibition in 1902. There were many variations of this design for floor or table lamps, with three, six, nine, or as many as 24 flower-head lamps clustered together.

The nautilus lamp design is also credited to Tiffany himself, the leaded glass shades copying the convoluted nautilus shape, which contained the light fitting and the bulb. His feeling for sculptural form found expression in bronze moulded to support or hold the shades.

The pond lily lamp was one of Tiffany's most inspired designs, the clustered flower shapes on slender stems rising from a sculptured lily pad base. The design won a Grand Prize at the Turin Exhibition of 1902.

ABOVE: A lily lamp, a Favrile vase and a Nautilus shell desk lamp, the shell neatly containing the light fitting and bulb.

LEFT: A pair of 3-light lily table lamps of Favrile gold glass and bronze.

RIGHT: **Floor-standing lamp of 12-light lily design. The lily light clusters are one of the most highly priced lamps today.**

The commercial aspect of Tiffany's work reached its climax with the lamps, which seized the public imagination. Very soon no home was complete without a Tiffany lamp, for they created interiors full of warmth and diffused light.

This was the first time Tiffany had produced items that were useful and practical, even if they were not essential to everyday life. Now the use of Favrile glass spread from flower vases and lamps to plaques, table decorations, cologne bottles, cups, plates and tobacco jars. He extended the range to enamels and paste, bronzes and mother of pearl for jewellery boxes, cigarette cases, pin cushions, bonbon dishes, vanity, snuff and cigarette boxes, toilet boxes and trays. His taste found expression in a thousand articles of applied art; these, occupying prominent places in households, exercised a happy influence on the taste of citizens according to Tiffany's creed.

"Yet the fact that things of daily use — lamps, flower vases, toilet articles reach a wider public than do paintings and sculpture — make the 'decorative' arts more important to a nation than the 'fine' arts," he said.

The vases and bowls made before 1896 when Tiffany first launched his new product on the market have a special elegance, and these early pieces, which were not meant for sale are not signed and numbered. The pieces first offered for sale had paper labels fixed to the base, though these labels have in most cases become detached. All the early pieces are distinctive, rare and highly prized today.

Once the product was launched on the market a numbering system was instituted. Tiffany later said: "Each article of Favrile glass is marked with the Tiffany name or initials, and all unusual pieces bear a number, the letters of the alphabet being used first as a prefix, later as a suffix to the numbers."

This system, which was coordinated with changes in the wording of the label in 1900, makes it possible to date Tiffany pieces accurately, according to Robert Koch. But other curators and writers have queried the system, pointing out anomalies and pieces that have no number, pieces that are signed in one of several ways and prized pieces marked "A-Coll", meant for Tiffany himself. Museums have noted the curious + sign on some pieces. These are on two pieces in the Victoria and Albert Museum, pieces which were bought from the Tiffany Regent Street shop. One piece, a swan-necked

OPPOSITE: **Tiffany designed these Samian red vases with Egyptian designs on the neck in tribute to the craft of ancient Samos.**

ABOVE: **All Tiffany's favourite nature themes appear in lamps. A design of autumn leaves (left) and dogwood (right).**

RIGHT: Tiffany paid particular attention to the base of lamps, realizing the scope they offered for artistic design. He opened a foundry and metal shop in 1897.

RIGHT: The Poinsettia Lamp — the appeal of Tiffany lamps was immediate, the public demand enormous. His team of artists kept up a constant flow of ideas to make each lamp individual and unique.

Persian perfume-sprinkler, is marked +1279 and dated 1896 in the inventory, price £3 14s 3d. The other, a green iridescent vase with "broad leaves alternating with pod-bearing stems in green and brown", is marked +2946 and has the label of Tiffany Glass and Decorating Company, with a price tag of $50. It was also bought at the Regent Street shop in 1896, price £10 6s 2d.

The numbering has yet to be fully deciphered and continues to baffle curators and collectors.

Samuel Bing exhibited Tiffany's Favrile glass at his new shop in Paris, La Maison de l'Art Nouveau. The shop's grand opening on 26 December, 1895 was the first representative exhibition of Art Nouveau and the 10 Tiffany windows with designs by French artists that Bing had commissioned were displayed, as well as some 20 pieces of Tiffany blown glass.

The windows caused much comment because they did not rely on the traditional methods of staining and etching designs into the glass. One critic described them as "transcriptions in American glass of a series of compositions by French artists", but another praised in particular the Ranson window by Tiffany, with its "fragments of various natural materials, transparent slices of pebbles or precious crystals. These split, cut and polished, give singular beauty to his work, with effects undreamed of by our forefathers."

The window by Bonnard appears to have been particularly beautiful, with mother and child depicted in lightly leaded outlines, marbled, striated, opalescent and iridescent glass building up the colour, form and perspective of the scene. Tiffany was to be known from this time onwards as the foremost American representative of Art Nouveau.

At this first Art Nouveau exhibition there were examples of glass by Gallé, jewellery by Lalique, paintings by Bonnard, Brangwyn, Pissarro and Toulouse-Lautrec, sculpture by Rodin, prints and drawings by Beardsley, Walter Crane and Whistler, posters and furniture. These artists all had the same creative urge to produce something truly new. They were all looking for a different inspiration, escaping from safe, imitative art.

Art Nouveau emerged in its various forms, now voluptuous and exuberant, now spare and angular. The lines were different and exciting: sensuous and flowing lines, lines that bent and curved and turned and did not conform, like women's flowing hair, twisting smoke, trailing leaves. These are

René Lalique's brilliance in glassmaking was different to
Tiffany's in that he was not so concerned with the colour
of the glass or the internal decoration. His graphic motifs
were moulded in relief, his characteristic glass was milky
blue opalescent or frosted — as seen in the vases (ABOVE)
and Suzanne au Bain c.1925 (RIGHT).

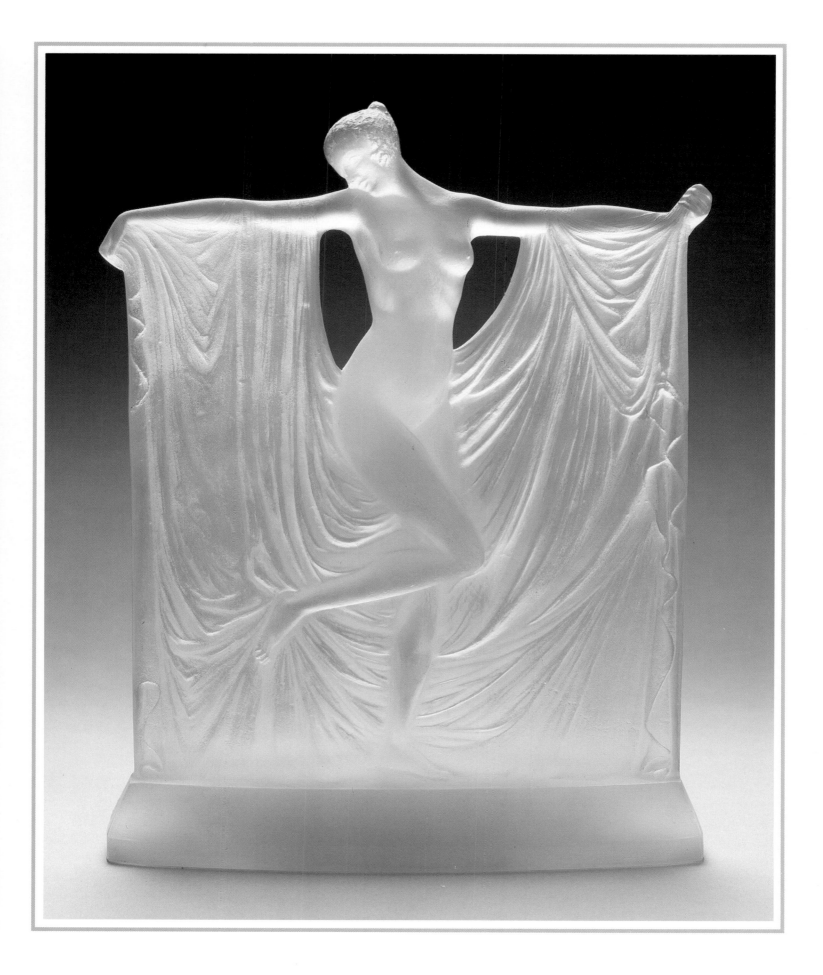

LEFT: **Small lattice-work bowl of cameo glass (left), paperweight glass decanter (centre) with marblized effect and a lustre vase of glowing colour abstract patterned.**

the lines of plant forms, growing boldly upwards on slender stems, drooping heavy flower heads, entwining branches. The lines could be as rounded as the female form, curving tenderly, or could reveal the explosive force of nature.

One of the most significant designs was an embroidered wall hanging, *Cyclamen*, designed by Hermann Obrist in 1895. It was described in the German magazine *Pan* so aptly that it became almost the signature of Art Nouveau: "Its frantic movement reminds us of the sudden violent curves occasioned by the crack of a whip; now appearing as a forceful outburst of the elements of nature, a stroke of lightning; now, as the defiant signature of a great man, a conqueror."

Art Nouveau produced different forms in different countries. It was sophisticated in France, with Lalique, who began his career designing jewellery. He was hailed as a revolutionary and creative inventor of luxury jewellery because of his use of non-precious materials such as glass, and he designed strange insects and stylized flowers with mysterious faces of women wreathed in flowing hair. He moved on from jewellery to enamels and to glass. Unlike Gallé and Tiffany, Lalique was not so concerned with the chemistry and colour of glass. His most characteristic glass was milky-blue opalescent, colourless and frosted, without internal decoration. His gift was in the poetic imagery of form in glass: nymphs curve their backs, maidens cavort, doves close their wings, wrens are poised for flight.

Lalique was able to simplify his technique to reach a wide public. The nymphs cavorted around vases, the birds were poised on ashtrays and perfume bottles, there was a vast range of household glassware produced by the Lalique factory in much the same way as Tiffany glass. Lalique was a household name that endured and was continued by his family.

Samuel Bing commissioned the young English artist Frank Brangwyn to cover the whole shop façade of La Maison de l'Art Nouveau with murals. The Czech artist Alfonse Mucha was also very much at the heart of the movement, with posters of Sarah Bernhardt. Scotland, despite its remoteness from Europe, emerged as one of the most interesting and important exponents of Art Nouveau, though the movement was largely ignored in England. Charles Rennie Mackintosh, architect, furniture designer and painter formed a famous group of four, exhibiting in Europe. This group rejected the curved

and florid overrich style and went for simplicity, long straight lines and sound structural form. Mackintosh's architectural masterpieces are all in and around Glasgow.

Spain produced its own genius in the Art Nouveau spirit, Antonio Gaudi, a man with extraordinary imagination and strong religious feelings. He simulated movement in architecture, confusing and exciting the eye. The curving lines of his buildings suggest the waves of the sea arrested in movement — and all in a revolutionary new building material, concrete.

From 1898 Tiffany took his place on the centre stage of the Art Nouveau scene. It was said that his blown glass "so attracted the attention of European connoisseurs that in many museums of Europe ... small collections were gathered together as object lessons for local craftsmen ... Tiffany's works were the first by an American artist to be known and imitated even in provincial regions of Europe."

The true genius of Tiffany emerged at this point and was recognized at its best, free of overrich and gaudy colour, free of representational figures. Cecilia Waern wrote in *The Studio* in 1897: "'Instances of contortion or intricacy are rare; the shapes are often capricious but with all the sweet waywardness of this exquisite material; they are almost invariably simpler, less slight, less tortured and more classical in the deepest sense, than the blown glass of Europe. They may recall shapes of Persia, Japan, Greece, because they have been *born* in the same way." There was something of abstract expressionist art in Tiffany's Favrile glass that was ahead of its time and only became fashionable half a century later. Overriding everything was Tiffany's love of colour and the shimmering changes of colour fused with light — rich, opulent and glowing. His colours are charged with emotion — the brilliant opalescent red, the subtle greens and peacock blues, the clear Attic aquamarine, the glowing, golden olive greens.

He believed that colour is to the eye as music to the ears, for, as Oscar Wilde said, music is the only art that is truly non-representational, and Tiffany came nearest to it with colour. Musical forms linked the artists of the Art Nouveau, with Whistler giving his pictures titles such as *Nocturne in Blue and White — Symphony in Green.* Music became visual as the colour and excitement of the *Ballets Russes* broke over Paris, composers like Stravinsky thought in

RIGHT: **Alphonse Mucha, with images of lovely languorous women, was one of the first exponents of Art Nouveau in Paris. This advertisement for Job cigarettes c.1900 produced a sense of shock at a time when it was considered very daring for a woman to smoke.**

LEFT: The Lotus Lamp of leaded glass with a bronze base has delicately coloured shade with a Far Eastern shape to it.

terms of colour, as designers such as Tiffany were thinking in abstract terms of music.

The spiritual strength of Tiffany's colour allied to movement and form is at its best in the vases made before 1900. There the colour harmonizes with the line, is subtle and delicate when he chooses, just as it is boldly glorious to suit other forms. His superiority as a colourist can clearly be seen when comparing his work with those who copied him. There were some who came close: in Europe, for example, copies were made by Johannes Loetz Witwe of Klostermuhle as early as 1897, with the trademark Loetz Austria, but the range was limited and the vases lacked the silky, tactile quality of Tiffany. Tiffany was forced to sue one competitor, Frederick Carder, who had copied Tiffany shapes and even achieved a velvet texture by spraying with stannous chloride. Carder established the Steuben Glassworks in Corning and registered his trademark as Steuben glass. Litigation was begun in 1913, but the matter was settled out of court. Later glass companies produced a vulgarized version of iridescent glass by spraying on the iridescence and calling it Carnival glass, a debasement of Tiffany's hard-won achievement.

The immense popularity of Tiffany Favrile glass and the day-to-day business of his organization left Tiffany little time for interior design projects, but some major schemes demanded his personal attention and in these he was to develop further his interest in mosaic.

Mosaic had interested him as far back as 1880 and for the next 10 years he experimented with his new variety of colours, used in minute pieces to form a picture or pattern. As the insatiable demand for Tiffany stained-glass windows continued and the praise for them rang in his ears, he began to assert that his windows were not for looking *through* but for looking *at*. They were not simply windows; they were works of art. Following from that, why should they be windows at all? Tiffany mosaics were designed on walls, like paintings. Many were produced over a period of 40 years, and were remarkable in their size and scope.

There was a mosaic for the Catholic cathedral of St Louis, Missouri, to a design by the Italian artist Aristide Leonari which spread over 27,870 square metres (300,000 square feet). Mosaics were used in the chapel designed for the 1893 World Fair in Chicago that created a sensation with its

LEFT: **Tel el Amama vases take their name from the site of the excavations of Pharaoh Akhenaten's capital in ancient Egypt and were inspired by the Egyptian vessels. Tiffany used a deep turquoise-blue opaque glass of a more brilliant blue than the Egyptian originals.**

ABOVE: Green and gold flowers form vases of graceful and delicate shape enhanced by the internal impression of leaves in the glass.

RIGHT: Opalescent and iridescent vases of Favrile glass. The flower form vases with their elegant attenuated lines and fragile petalled shapes are the peak of Tiffany's achievement. He had a team of glass blowers, headed by Arthur Nash, who could produce such pieces.

Byzantine richness. Mosaic featured specially in the Fifth Avenue home of millionaire Henry O. Havemeyer, who insisted on personal attention.

With the Havemeyer residence Tiffany surprised his critics again with a fresh, unexpected creative approach. The eclectic mixture of ornaments, hanging lamps, Oriental and Islamic splendour was restrained now, for he had a more mature grasp of harmonies. There were sensational features — the amazing hanging staircase, the white mosaic hall, the library ceiling hung with a mosaic of multicoloured silk, the pillared entrance, the Japanese lacquers — but they were a unified whole. Tiffany skilfully created interiors that were a setting for Havemeyer's collection of paintings, works by Rembrandt, El Greco and Manet.

Mrs Havemeyer was thrilled with the result, specially the hanging staircase, derived from the Doge's Palace in Venice. Others too, were breathless with admiration.

Tiffany followed this success with another major project, the design and installation of a memorial window for the new library at Yale University. The window was donated by Samuel B. Chittendon of Brooklyn in memory of his daughter, Mary Lusk, the wife of William T. Lusk, Tiffany's personal physician. The window was 9×1.5m (30×5ft) and Tiffany incorporated 20 figures into the design, linking them in a repetitive decorative motif.

As was now the accepted custom, there was praise on all sides for Tiffany: "No-one can stand in this room without a profound feeling of satisfaction that America produces such window works as that of Louis Tiffany. It is a truly wonderful production of this man of thought."

The colossal glass drop-curtain at the National Theatre in the Palace of Fine Arts in Mexico City demonstrated the sheer splendour of Tiffany's work in mosaic. This commission involved a model produced by the painter and stage designer Harry Stoner, a landscape panorama of the view from the presidential palace with snowcapped mountain peaks. It was translated by Tiffany's team at the Corona factory into a glass mosaic of 167 square metres (1,800 square feet) containing almost a million tesserae and weighing some 27 tons. It went on display in New York before being shipped to Mexico City, where it was built into a finely engineered construction that took only seconds to raise and lower.

RIGHT: Intaglio cut-glass vases (left and right) with decoration of green vine leaves on clear glass Rock crystal vase with trailing leaf decoration (centre).

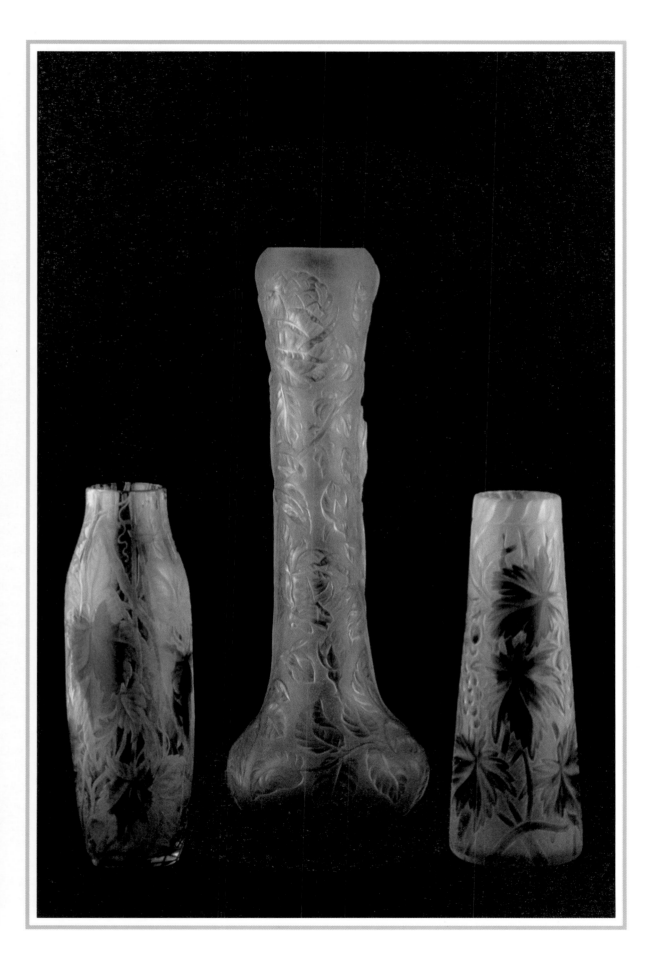

LEFT: The Wistaria table,
item no. 342 in the
original catalogue at $350,
is now one of the most
highly prized Tiffany
lamps.

ABOVE: A sophisticated
bronze and glass filigree
table lamp.

ABOVE: The Daffodil
Lamp on a bronze base,
the heads of the daffodils
forming the border of the
shade.

Audiences in Mexico were given a luxury of applied art unknown to opera and theatre goers in London, Paris and New York, thanks to the enlightened rule of President Diaz and the genius of Tiffany, as he said himself. The fire curtain was a thick wall separating stage from auditorium. It was like a vast window, square-mullioned with a landscape beyond of flowers, lakes, pastures, hills, a mountain range, volcanoes and the snowy caps of Popocatépetl and Ixtaccihuatl, with the clouds of sunset above. The colour was wrought in mosaic and the illusion helped by illumination.

The immediate result for Tiffany was a commission for a mosaic for the Curtis Publishing Company — a glass vista for their new building in Philadelphia. The building was almost complete, but there was no mural for the large place which clearly demanded one. Tiffany was eager to undertake the project but no adequate sketch for the mural could be found.

Edward Bok, editor of *Ladies' Home Journal,* had commissioned three artists successively to make a design for the mural, but each had died before producing a sketch. He then organized a competition of muralists but eventually rejected all their offerings. In his book *The Americanization of Edward Bok,* Bok describes how he recalled Maxfield Parrish, the artist, telling him of a dream garden he would like to construct at his summer home.

> Bok took Parrish to Mr Tiffany's studio; the two artists talked together, the glass-worker showed the canvas-painter his work, with the result that the two became enthusiastic to co-operate in trying the experiment.
> Parrish agreed to make a sketch for Mr Tiffany's approval and within six months, after a number of conferences and an equal number of sketches, they were ready to begin work. Bok only hoped both artists would outlive their commissions.

When completed, the resulting mosaic was 15 metres long and 4.6 metres high (49 feet long and 15 feet high). Over 7,000 people filed past it and admired it. Both artists lived to see the day and the *Dream Garden* was applauded for many years to come. It is still part of the Curtis Publishing House building in Philadelphia, although its proprietors have changed.

Tiffany declared that only glass could have done justice to the artist's dream garden. Never inhibited by modesty, Tiffany said:

In translating this painting so that its poetical and luminous idealism should find its way even to the comparatively uneducated eye, the medium used is of supreme importance, and it seemed impossible to secure the effect desired on canvas and with paint. In glass, however, selecting the lustrous, the transparent, the opaque and the opalescent, and each with its own texture, a result is secured which does illustrate the mystery, and it tells the story, giving play to imagination, which is the message it seeks to convey.

As a matter of fact, it is practically a new art. Never before has it been possible to give the perspective in mosaics as it is shown in this picture, and the most remarkable and beautiful effect is secured when different lights play upon this completed mosaic.

It will be found that the mountains recede, the trees and foliage stand out distinctly, and, as the light changes, the purple shadows will creep slowly from the base of the mountain to its top; that the canyons and the waterfalls, the thickets and the flowers, all tell their story and interpret Mr Parrish's dream.

I trust it may stand in the years to come for a development in glass making and its application to art which will give students a feeling that in this year of nineteen hundred and fifteen something worthy has been produced for the benefit of mankind, and that it may serve as an incentive to others to carry even farther the true mission of the mosaic.

The *Dream Garden* glass mosaic made in 1915 for the Curtis Publishing Company after a design by Maxfield Parrish. Only glass, Tiffany said, could do justice to the artist's vision of a dream garden.

# FADING GLORY

"Break in small pieces that Tiffany screen."

PRESIDENT THEODORE ROOSEVELT

THE TURN OF THE CENTURY was the time when Tiffany brought his art glass to its highest peak of creative brilliance. The 1900 Paris Exposition was a triumph for him and for Art Nouveau. He was then 52 and he was world-famous.

The enormous Paris Exposition came at a very exciting time, when great scientific advances were being made — motion pictures, escalators, wireless telegraphy, the engineering feat of the Eiffel Tower, the discovery of radium. The bewildering rate of scientific advances was matched by an almost feverish creativity in the arts, and at the exhibition the exuberant imaginative displays of the Art Nouveau movement made their greatest impact.

Tiffany father and son were showered with honours. Louis Tiffany was created a Chevalier de la Legion d'Honneur and won a Gold Medal; his father's firm, Tiffany & Co, won three Grand Prix, 10 gold, 10 silver and two Bronze Medals. Clara Driscoll won a prize for the dragonfly Tiffany lamp.

As president of the Tiffany Glass and Decorating Company, Louis Tiffany was artistic director of over 100 skilled workers. He could design and experiment and still keep tight control of work at the studios and at the Corona factory.

He was regarded as a good employer, liked and respected. He was evidently a perfectionist; he knew what he wanted and was often exasperating in his determination to get it. But he was willing and able to show how it could be achieved, and he was generous with praise and encouragement as well as criticism.

He was remarkable in giving opportunities to women at that time, training women workers, encouraging them to try their skills and take an active part in the business. Mrs Clara Driscoll, designer of the dragonfly lamp, came to work for him in 1887 and was trained as a designer by him, becoming one of the highest-paid women workers in the United States in her time, earning more than $10,000 a year.

Tiffany paid good salaries, but he was strict about advances. Employees who got into debt, or bought on credit, could find themselves dismissed. Tiffany had learned a hard lesson himself over his Lyceum Theater venture and had seen his friend Steel McKaye come to a tragic end because of credit failure.

But this never put Tiffany off the theatre. The theatrical world fascinated him and during his busiest times the theatre, in its heyday throughout the Gay Nineties, was his favourite form of entertainment and leisure. He only expressed regret that his wife, did not enjoy going as much as he did. He seems to have felt a natural

ABOVE: **After 1900 Tiffany Studios began to expand into producing a wide range of tableware, which was very popular for wedding presents, such as these Favrile glass goblets.**

affinity with the actor on stage who gave a creative performance, bringing joy and beauty into the lives of strangers. Tiffany's creative output was like a theatrical performance for others to appreciate, applaud — or criticize.

Tiffany as a family man appears to have been a fond tyrant. His second wife, Louise, was a quiet and devout woman, giving much of her time to working for charity. She was devoted to him, showing great affection to the children from his first marriage as well as to her own three daughters, twins, Julia and Comfort, and the youngest, Dorothy. She never interfered in his business.

His father, Charles L. Tiffany was a vigorous 88 and still directing the affairs of the jewellers and silversmiths Tiffany & Co. He was evidently proud of Louis Tiffany's achievements and continued to encourage his son to expand and take on new challenges, as he had throughout his life.

Of Louis Tiffany's three older children, Charles L. Tiffany II, as the only grandson, was being groomed to take over Tiffany & Co from his grandfather in due course — a role he was not resisting as his father had done. He graduated from Yale in 1900. The elder daughter, Mary, married Graham Lusk, son of the Tiffany family physician; the younger, Hilda, suffered from tuberculosis, the disease that had caused her mother's early death.

Tiffany seems to have enjoyed more relaxation at this time. He had acquired a country estate, The Briars, on Long Island, and here he was content to organize the gardens and return to the pleasures of painting. It is said that he also liked to read aloud from articles in current periodicals when they made flattering references to him and his work.

The Briars, a country house in the Colonial style, was decorated by Tiffany in a simpler style than his studio. The woodwork was lighter, the ornamentation more

LEFT: **Nautilus shell desk lamp and a bronze mounted opalescent glass frame.**

restrained, frieze decorations were simplified, the leaded glass used for doors and windows was in a pattern of abstract rectangles. The furniture was produced under Tiffany's supervision and photographs is surprisingly modern.

It was a happy place for Tiffany to relax with his family and, from 1901, his first grandson, William T. Lusk. That year was also a happy one as he was chosen as decorator for the Yale Bicentennial. He had always been a little self-conscious about his lack of college education, but he had kept close associations with Yale, and his son enrolled there. The decoration of orange Japanese lanterns, blue flags and evergreens in the campus was very effective and Yale showed its appreciation by awarding Tiffany an honorary degree.

His artistic achievements were marked with more awards into the new century in Europe and America, and ever increasing sales. This was the Tiffany art industry in full swing, and the production was prodigious.

Prices were high — $750, for example, for one of the large lamps — and Tiffany's methods of retailing were unusual in that he set the prices on a strictly sale or return basis; the glass remained his property. He did not sell to shops and stores; he supplied the glass for them to sell, the retailer taking commission on the sale. If the glass was unsold after three months it was returned to the factory; if it failed to be sold by three different retailers, it would be given away, discounted, often destroyed.

As sales continued to increase, the Corona factory expanded to become Tiffany Furnaces. The Tiffany Glass and Decorating Company became Tiffany Studios. Arthur Nash was now assisted by his two sons, Douglas and Leslie, and Dr Parker McIllhiney led a team of chemists.

Tiffany Furnaces was devoted to the production of glass and glass objects, while Tiffany Studios began to expand after 1900 into all the various sectors of interior

RIGHT: Favrile glass used for a bell lamp (right) and for a whole range of interior decorating and household objects, such as this inkwell (left).

decoration and household objects. The decorating service of Tiffany Studios carried a full line of Oriental rugs and fabrics for upholstery and curtains in patterns that harmonized with Tiffany glassware. An enamelling department was set up and Tiffany provided sketches for enamel work to be carried out by a small unit, with Julia Munsen in charge, using models from his great collection of Oriental and Islamic *objets d'art*, Chinese cloisonné and Japanese sword guards.

Enamels were exhibited at the Buffalo, New York Exhibition of 1901 and much admired for their astonishing range of colours, from translucent to opaque. Another range of vitreous enamel work was undertaken, ground glass being applied to metal objects and fired in the furnace until the glass fused to the metal to create an iridescent effect. The metal objects were made in the Corona foundry in copper, brass or bronze and ranged from small vases and ornamental boxes to lamp bases.

After 1900 Tiffany Studios produced desk sets in glass and bronze and enamel inlaid with glass or mother of pearl in many different patterns, ash trays, tableware, ceramic lamp bases, cigarette boxes and lighters, inkstands, jardinières, clocks, photograph frames, pin cushions, decanters, cologne bottles, goblets, plates,

plaques and dishes. Some pottery pieces were made, but the pottery produced could not match the beauty of the glass and was discontinued.

Favrile glass dinner services were very popular and became fashionable as wedding presents. Matched sets of 48 pieces were produced in a dozen related shapes, in gold or blue iridescent glass, sometimes engraved in a grapevine design.

Tiffany also tried his hand at jewellery, for, as he said, "a painter born with a sense of color must revel in the deep set richness of precious gems, love the tones in marbles, onyx, malachite and carnelian, in various shells, in pearly opals, and coral, in old amber and tortoiseshell."

Also, of course, he had access to the stones and gems amassed by Tiffany & Co, and there were a great variety and a wealth of material to choose from. Some very fine pieces were produced: for example, a peacock necklace with a mosaic centre-piece of opals, amethysts and sapphires and a pendant below of a single large ruby.

At the Paris Salon of 1906 some notable Tiffany pieces were shown with a distinctly Art Nouveau form: for example, a dragonfly hatpin set with opals on platinum, dandelions and blackberries of opals. One brooch, described as "a marine motif, half crab, half octopus with writhing feet", attracted particular praise. Some of his most attractive designs were based on wild flowers: a favourite was the "charming weed", as he called it, wild carrot or queen's lace, the small white flowers with a garnet at the centre and a lace of white enamel on silver.

About 1895 it had become the fashion to mix precious, semiprecious and worthless materials in making jewellery, with some notable success by Lalique, but the fashion only lasted for about 15 years.

Tiffany's jewellery was very expensive to make as so much time was spent on it and financially it was not a success. Jewellery production ceased in 1916.

On the death of his father in February 1902, it became necessary for Louis to give more time and attention to the affairs of Tiffany & Co. He became artistic director and vice-president, with Charles T. Cook as president.

All the glass-making departments of Tiffany Studios were then moved to an impressive building on the corner of Madison Avenue and 45th Street, where they remained until 1918, and later in the same year Tiffany purchased a property called Laurelton Hall. It was an old-fashioned hotel with 580 acres at Oyster Bay, Long Island, made famous by Fenimore Cooper. It had a long shoreline facing Cold Spring Harbor and there Tiffany planned a new mansion for himself.

The Tiffany art industry was in full swing in the early
years of the 20th century and there was great demand for
everything they produced. It was always artistic and high
quality, such as this jardinière.

LEFT: Many tried to copy Favrile glass but none could achieve the glowing depth of colour and the technical brilliance shown here in paperweight and millefiori glass.

RIGHT: Samplers of Tiffany Mosaic glass for the Citizens Bank. Ohio and for the First National Bank.

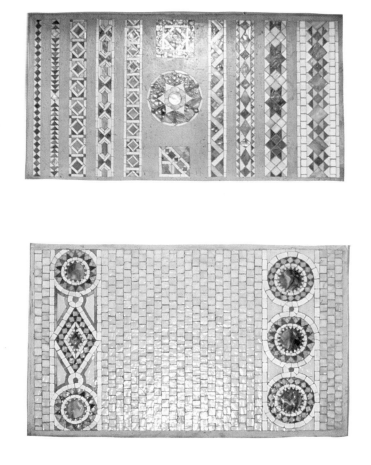

The hotel was demolished and Tiffany set about designing the house, the gardens and the interior to make it the showpiece of the century, unlike anything seen before or since.

At Laurelton Hall he was owner, architect and designer all in one, so he could carry out his own bold ideas without restraint. He began by modelling the landscape and the elevations in clay and wax. The layout of the steelframe building was asymmetrical with a small stream running through the centre of an enclosed court, watched over by an immense Japanese bronze dragon. Visitors were immediately impressed by the fountain, water bubbling from a glass jar in the shape of a Greek amphora which changed colour in a magical way with the effect of sunlight and running water.

Approached from the drive, a bell tower came first into view, with the main entrance at an upper level between columns of granite and ceramic mosaics. The bell tower pealed the Westminster chimes. Blue iridescent tiles on the lintel provided a recurring colour note, repeated in the domed skylight over the central court. In all there were 84 rooms and 25 bathrooms, and a high terrace overlooked Cold Spring Harbor where there was a private yacht basin.

From the shore the house appeared mushroom-shaped, like a mosque, rounded copper roofing the house and the tower. Its daring, unconventional shape had some resemblance to the work of the architect Gaudi in Spain. It was a major Art Nouveau achievement in America, quite unique, and it became the most publicized home in the United States, with frequent illustrated features singing its praises. Many of these features were written at Tiffany's instigation.

By all accounts and from the photographs of Laurelton Hall it would appear that the synthesis of structure and form was not wholly achieved; the styling was

LEFT TOP: **The mansion at Oyster Bay, Lon Island had a high terrace overlooking Cold Spring Harbour.**

BELOW: **At Laurelton Hall Tiffany was owner, architect and designer all in one, so he could carry out his bold ideas without restraint.**

somewhat heavy-handed. Either side of the central court were the living room and dining room, designed as a light room and a dark room, an idea Tiffany had introduced for the Chicago Fair chapel in 1893.

The light room was the most successful, its dignified simple style one of the best of Tiffany's interiors. The dining room stretched the whole width of the house; the colours were light and fresh, clear plate-glass from floor to frieze let in the daylight, the furnishings were simple and sparse, and the ornament restrained. There was a rectangular fireplace faced with green marble and a mantel with three clocks, one for the day of the week, one for the hours of the day, one for the days of the month. An outdoor-indoor effect was achieved with a glass-enclosed verandah — partly clear glass, partly stained glass with a wistaria design.

The living room, dimly lit, featured Tiffany's stained glass which he had saved for display in his own home. *Feeding the Flamingoes* from the Chicago Fair; his *Four Seasons* window, cut into separate panels and set into the wall; *Flowers, Fish and Fruit*, designed in 1885; *Eggplants*, from 1880. Later he added the largest window, *The Bathers*, intended for exhibition in San Francisco but withdrawn by Tiffany because he was not satisfied with the lighting arrangements.

ABOVE: Laurelton Hall was a major achievement of Art
Nouveau design and it became the most publicized home
in the United States.

ABOVE: Tiffany displayed his stained-glass masterpieces
at Laurelton Hall. *The Bathers* appeared to fine effect
in an alcove of the living room.

The living room had a cave-like fireplace with a bearskin rug and there were heavy iron lighting fixtures in turtleback style. The cornices curved into the ceiling.

There were also rooms for his American Indian collections, an octagonal Chinese room for the Oriental antiques, tea rooms, a music room and a palm house full of exotic plants. The overall effect was theatrical and a bit overpowering, like a dream fantasy. The estate was valued at half a million dollars in 1908. There were many delays in the completion of the house because Tiffany kept making additions. There were disputes over the beach rights with the previous owner and squabbles over electricity, which was cut off from the Tiffany property at one stage. The neighbours, who included Theodore Roosevelt, did not take kindly to Tiffany's plans and several seem to have suspected him of affairs with their wives.

Louise, the second Mrs Tiffany, died before the house was finished. Once again Tiffany found himself with children at home and no mother. His twin daughters, Julia and Comfort, were 17, Dorothy was 13. Tiffany gave his daughter Mary and her husband, Graham Lusk, The Briars as their home, and the three Lusk children grew up there.

On the death of his first wife Tiffany had plunged into risky theatrical ventures and fast company. Now he seemed to turn to a theatrical lifestyle, organizing grandiose events, entertaining lavishly and extravagantly. From this date he became notably more eccentric. He sought the limelight in public and became a tyrant at home, ruling his daughters' lives protectively, taking them on long holidays abroad to distract them from boyfriends he disliked.

There was a good deal of talk about Tiffany's association with married women, particularly with the wife of his chemist. Stanford White, an old friend from his theatrical past, became involved with a teenage actress and was shot dead by her husband in jealous fury at a performance in the Madison Square Theater.

Tiffany's reaction was to guard his daughters ever more jealously, but despite the cruises, the tennis parties and the lavish garden fêtes he arranged for them, they each left home. Julia married Gordon Parks in 1910, Comfort married Robert de Kay Gilder in 1911 and Dorothy married Dr Robert Burlingham in 1914. Their departure and his grief at Hilda's death from tuberculosis in 1908 left Tiffany very lonely in his magnificent mansion.

There was a new note of criticism of his work from about 1903, when an article appeared in *The Craftsman*.

> The name of Tiffany promised us an admirable display, but we must confess to have been deeply disappointed ... There is absolutely nothing to observe among these pieces — heavy, yet weak in form and with vivid, yet inharmonious coloring ... We are indeed far from the exquisite specimens of Mr Tiffany's earlier manner, in which the gamut of rich golds sang so superbly. We trust that the artist may return to his first method.

It had become noticeable that the creation of individual unique objects had been reduced. The production of matched sets of place settings, desk sets, lamps and lighting fixtures, vases and bowls in fine materials and popular designs was sufficient in Tiffany's view to maintain his position as the world's foremost industrial artist.

He was the victim of his own success and he was doing too much. He was preoccupied with the output of Tiffany Studios, the Corona factory and also of Tiffany & Co since his father's death. His great schemes and all the problems concerned with Laurelton Hall absorbed his attention.

More and more he was having to rely on other designers to come up with ideas for the glass-makers, for his output was in great demand. But he was losing some of his most talented staff as they left and set up in competition. He was still winning awards and prizes at American exhibitions, but he wanted more than this.

He never doubted his own values, but he was becoming impatient with the inability of the American critics and populace to grasp his concepts of beauty. He made strenuous efforts to educate public taste, and at the same time promoted his own work.

In 1910 he delivered his first public lecture in an effort to impress influential people, speaking on "The Tasteful Use of Light and Color in Artificial Illumination" at Johns Hopkins University. But he was not cut out for the scholarly approach and was never at his ease with words. Theatrical spectacle appealed to him more. He decided to make himself better known as an

Sulphur Crested Cockatoos, the glass mosaic exhibition piece in the Haworth Art Gallery, Accrington, Lancashire. It is traditionally attributed to Joseph Briggs, Tiffany's right-hand man.

arbiter of taste and upholder of artistic values, with entertainment and lavish spectacle that would be long remembered as an aesthetic experience of the most superior kind.

The splendour of Ancient Egypt was re-created under the direction of Joseph Lindon Smith, an artist who was preserving the treasures of the ancient past discovered in recent archaeological excavations. Tiffany himself, magnificently turbaned as an Egyptian potentate, supervized the catering by Delmonico's and mingled with his guests at the 72nd Street mansion. A stage was set up in the Madison Avenue showrooms for a masque. Ruth St Denis, in a very short skirt, performed an East Indian nautch dance to music specially composed by Thomas Steinway and played by members of the Philharmonic concealed in the wings. Favrile vases were arranged on stage but seemed not related to the cavortings of the various dancers. Performers in the masque were members of the family and "socialite amateurs" doing their best.

*The New York Times* described it as "the most lavish costume fête ever seen in New York". But Tiffany's ethos of beauty was turned into revelry as the champagne flowed. The young socialites enjoyed the wild party but were not so receptive to his aesthetic principles. It was the social columnists who raved over the party, not the art critics.

At the same time as features were appearing in the newspapers illustrating Tiffany's Egyptian fête, there were reports of the famous Armory Show exhibition. The public saw there for the first time the works of Matisse, the Fauves, the Cubists and the German Expressionists, and the exhibition was a sensation.

It was a highly significant art exhibition. Tiffany was shocked and confused by it, seeing in its ugliness a rejection of all his own values. He saw his life as a constant quest for beauty: "If the ugly is there I don't look at it." Here were artists deliberately turning the human figure into geometric cubes, expressing movement with angular lines and sharp, spare images — and being praised for it.

He was disconcerted to find that so many leading American artists were included, that the artist Arthur B. Davies, whose paintings he admired was in charge, yet he himself had not been asked to participate.

He told himself that it could not be important, as he had had no part in it, and yet the feeling that he had been left out and left behind was inevitable and hard to accept. Feeling threatened, he spoke out against "these modernists", unaware that the shock he had received from their work was comparable with the sensation he himself had created with his unorthodox treatment of colour, glass and form in his day.

He could not accept that his day was over. As he felt the tide of fashion turning against him, his own reaction became more extreme, vigorously he defended his life's work in more and more extravagant terms. He must promote the concepts he believed in, for they justified his whole career.

In 1911 he selected 150 truly intellectual gentlemen, who possessed the quality of genius like himself, and invited them to Laurelton Hall to "inspect the spring flowers". They were brought by special train and served a feast of peacocks by young ladies dressed in Ancient Greek costumes and carrying live peacocks on their shoulders. After dinner they witnessed a spectacle of light and music, with Bach, Beethoven and Brahms played on the organ. The event was dignified this time, but it was not enough. It was only a temporary distraction, soon overshadowed by events in Europe.

Tiffany decided on something more permanent: a record of his achievements, a memorial volume. The volume, *The Art Work of Louis C. Tiffany* must come under the heading of vanity publishing, for it was published at Tiffany's expense by Doubleday, Page & Co., in a limited edition of 502 copies on parchment. The book was never sold: only 300 were distributed to those Tiffany considered deserving. A copy was sent to the British Museum in 1916.

The text of the book consists of a series of interviews in which Tiffany dictated his views to Charles de Kay, under headings he himself chose: Tiffany the Painter, Tiffany the Maker of Stained Glass, A Builder of Homes, As Landscape Architect, and so on. The illustrations show Tiffany in the princely surroundings of Laurelton Hall and examples of his work. Very little mention is made of family, friends, business associates, other artists or, the craftsmen who worked with him. The false modesty of the foreword he wrote, declaring the book was written for his children and at their request, is said to have been a standing joke.

Yet as with much so-called vanity publishing, *The Art Work of Louis C. Tiffany* puts in permanent form a valuable personal document that gives the reader today a unique insight into the life of the artist. Tiffany's strong personality comes through, his burning quest for beauty as he understands it finds expression, and one cannot but sympathize with his hurt pride and admire the positive and determined way he is driven to defend his own work because he has not changed and fashion is fickle.

He concludes on a ringing note with this tribute to himself: "When we think of the silent effect produced in a thousand families and in more museums than could easily be named by the inspiring art work he has produced we can say sincerely that he has deserved well of the republic." Noble as Othello, and deeply wronged.

He had been very fortunate in his timing at many points in his career, but now the times were against him. The harsh realities of war, the terrible slaughter on the battlefields of France and Belgium, had produced a post-war rejection of the flamboyant extravagances and the gilded artefacts of the turn of the century. The bizarre fantasies and creative imaginings of the Art Nouveau epoch were seen as decadent. The roaring Twenties roared to a different kind of frenzy. The world had become more austere.

The richly gilded, colourful stained glass of Tiffany's heyday was being rejected on all sides. His gloriously Byzantine chapel, built for the World's Fair in 1893, then installed in the Cathedral of St John the Divine, was sealed off in darkness by instruction of the architect Ralph Adam Cram. Years earlier Cram had designed the Russel Sale Memorial Chapel on Long Island and planned to put clear glass in the neo-gothic windows — but instead a Tiffany design was accepted. Appointed as architect for the Cathedral of St John the Divine refurbishment, Cram took his revenge. Tiffany removed the chapel and displayed it instead at Laurelton Hall.

Already his famous White House screen had fallen from favour. President Theodore Roosevelt told the architect Charles F. McKim, who was in charge of remodelling the White House in the neo-classical manner, to "break in small pieces that Tiffany screen". Tiffany had no opportunity to remove it to Laurelton Hall.

He continued to live a life of luxury and extravagance. He had amassed a

fortune, by his own efforts; only a small part of his income came from his position in his father's firm. He paid his way always, abhorred debt of any kind, and felt that the way he spent his money was his own affair and that what he did brought pleasure to others. He spent the summers in Europe, often escorting groups of his favourite employees to places of interest in England, France and Germany. He liked the German people particularly, admiring their industry and efficiency, and often still expressed this opinion when America and Germany were at war.

In February 1916 he planned another lavish spectacle with a view to his own self-glorification. He again asked the artist Joseph Lindon Smith to create a fantasy for his birthday which would be sure to be "featured in the press as the artistic sensation of the social season".

In staging this birthday masque, *The Quest of Beauty*, an allegory symbolizing Tiffany's career, the difficulties Smith encountered have been recorded by his widow, Corinna Lindon Smith. The masque as a symphonic poem was visualized played to soft musical accompaniment, with 45 characters and changing colour effects with a new system of "dome lighting". Some 33 reds were used instead of the standard six, she says. There were no difficulties over the costs, though; lighting alone cost $15,000.

Tiffany promised the leading roles in the masque, Fire and Beauty, to two of his protégées, a première *danseuse* of the ballet of the Metropolitan Opera and an actress soon to make her debut on Broadway. Inevitably there was a clash of personalities and egos.

As a climax a huge bowl of iridescent blown glass was shown to contain Beauty's daughter representing a pearl. The masque was said to be a stupendous triumph, cheered to the echo, talked about for decades.

Tiffany, in a speech to his birthday guests, talked about his own quest for beauty, defended Art Nouveau and poured scorn on the new style of art that was taking its place.

The "Modernists" as they are called for want of a better term — I mean Cubists, Futurists etc — wander after curiosities of technique, vaguely hoping they may light on some invention which will make them famous. They do not belong to art, they are not artists; they are untrained inventors of processes of the arts.

Tiffany was, in fact, an example of what had happened to Art Nouveau. The 1900 Exhibition was at once the climax and the finale of it. At that time only the small circle of wealthy influential people who could afford the high prices of unique created objects or small limited editions were part of it. Once it became popular and available to a wider public and had to be produced in large quantities, the vigour and exuberance were diluted and a deterioration of design set in. As cheapened versions of the originals were produced, the wheel came full circle, the very vulgarization that Art Nouveau had been created to combat overtook Art Nouveau itself and the boldest designers began to experiment in new directions.

Influential figures retired from the scene. Samuel Bing retired in 1902; his Maison de l'Art Nouveau in Paris became simply a gallery for Far Eastern art and antiquities, the way it had begun. Emile Gallé died in Nancy in 1904.

During the First World War Tiffany, in the splendour of Laurelton Hall had found his consolation in contemplating the beauty he had collected and created that was displayed all about him. He began to work out a plan, a scheme originally suggested by Oscar Wilde, of a school of rational art in America with a museum attached: "not one of those dreadful modern institutions where there is a stuffed and very dusty giraffe and a case or two of fossils, but a place where are gathered examples of art decoration from various periods and countries".

The special museum school became a reality in 1918 when the Louis Comfort Tiffany Foundation was set up with a substantial endowment for art education and Laurelton Hall as a retreat for students and artists. The trustees included Louis Tiffany and his son, Charles. Chairman and first president was Robert de Forest, an old associate, then director of the Metropolitan Museum of Art. Stanley Lothrop was appointed as resident director of the Foundation.

Nineteen approved students began their non-academic art education based on Tiffany's principle of art-by-absorption in 1920. In Europe at about the same time Walter Gropius was opening the reorganized Weimar Art School and some 500 students began training in the Staatliches Bauhaus. To Gropius "art was not a branch of science which can be learned step by step, from a book", a sentiment with which Tiffany would have agreed.

RIGHT: **Brilliantly coloured mosaic section of iridescent glass tesserae, rescued from the Philadelphia Mint.**

A large percentage of the young men and women who became resident members at Laurelton Hall continued in art, craft and design careers. Among them was Hugh McKean, who has recorded his appreciation of the encouragement and assistance given to the young artists. The fascinating unreality of Laurelton Hall appealed to him, but he did not realize until later how Laurelton Hall was actually a modern house, way ahead of its time.

> We had nothing to do all day except to work where and how we wished on our art, and at night we sat down to dinner to be served by two rather elegant butlers. Every Saturday morning at eleven o'clock we assembled in the gallery, along with our latest work. A magnificent old car [a 1911 Crane] would come whirling into the courtyard, a little dog with fantastic jumping ability would hop out — and then Mr Tiffany, frail and benign. His face was always radiant with smiles and kindness and he seemed to be pleased at the happiness he was giving all of us.

Tiffany would walk round the gallery, sitting down abruptly anywhere at all because he knew Mr Lothrop, the director of the Foundation, would always have a chair ready right behind him. He would study the pictures, discuss the importance of beauty and give gentle words of encouragement to the young artists.

"But his real thoughts were revealed, I thought," says Hugh McKean, "when he would say often at the end of his visit that paintings should not 'hurt the eye'."

Tiffany continued to oversee various projects, and the last major commission was the decoration of the Presidential Palace in Havana, Cuba. The furnishings were mainly period reproductions but included 23 Tiffany rugs and 15 Tiffany lamps. The Metropolitan Museum acquired a Tiffany landscape window in 1925, probably at the suggestion of Robert de Forest, still serving as its director.

The building that housed Tiffany Studios at 345 Madison Avenue was sold at the time the Art Foundation was launched, moving to smaller showrooms in Madison Avenue and then finally to 46 West 23rd Street. The

production of collectors' items ceased after the war. When the entire stock was offered at a clearance sale in 1920, many items in the stock had been unsold for many years.

Tiffany Furnaces was under the management of A. Douglas Nash from 1919, when Arthur Nash retired, and production was soon curtailed. The market was then being flooded with Carnival glass, mass-produced by being pressed or moulded and then dipped to give a thin coating of pale iridescence. Tiffany, whose name had been synonymous with iridescent glass, withdrew his financial support from Tiffany Furnaces, because of the increasing commercialization, he said, and within a few months the production of Favrile glass ceased for ever.

Joseph Briggs remained in charge of the retail organization, selling off the stocks still held, but in 1932 Briggs filed a petition for bankruptcy. The firm managed to struggle on for a few more years, but it was a sad end to the high ideals of Louis Comfort Tiffany, its creator. To Joseph Briggs went the task of disposing of the remaining stock, at various auctions, for a small fraction of its cost price.

Tiffany had always been energetic and egocentric, claiming the limelight yet oddly inhibited by an acute shyness that made it difficult for him to communicate, even with family and close friends. This characteristic became more and more marked and he seems to have lived like a recluse in his eighties, neglected, disappointed, his work regarded as irrelevant by the art world of the day.

His only companion was Sarah Hanley. She had gone to Laurelton Hall to nurse Tiffany through a kidney illness. He persuaded her to stay on and she became his protégée. A girl from a simple background, talking in a strong Irish brogue, she stayed by Tiffany, calling him Padre and wearing yellow, his favourite colour. Under his influence she became a painter, exemplifying the osmosis effect that Tiffany believed in so ardently, and her work was exhibited. She accompanied Tiffany on painting trips to Florida, visited exhibitions with him and remained his constant companion until his death in 1933.

He died on 17 January, a month before his eighty-fifth birthday, mourned by few, forgotten by many.

# KITSCH OR GENIUS?

"I have always striven to fix beauty in wood or stone, or glass or pottery, in oil or water-color, by using whatever seemed fittest for the expression of beauty; that has been my creed, and I see no reason to change it."

LOUIS C. TIFFANY

TIFFANY'S NAME FADED INTO OBSCURITY; the beautiful things he had created were discarded; the stock of Tiffany Studios was sold. It was sad that he died when his reputation was in eclipse, he himself forgotten and neglected, his work treated with derision. The silence continued for many years after his death and the records of his achievements were destroyed.

The 72nd Street mansion, where he lived and died, was razed to the ground to make way for an apartment house in 1938, and the same year the remaining stock of Tiffany Studios, some 1,100 items, was auctioned off — paintings, fabrics, rugs, chandeliers, pottery, furniture and some 20 Tiffany windows.

Joseph Briggs disposed of the remainder of the glassware. Details of these sales are not available, but it seems that the auctions were held at intervals over several years and achieved very low prices. The last remaining items were consigned to the rubbish tips of New York.

Briggs had assembled his own collection of Tiffany art glass and in 1933, when he returned to England for the last time, he gave half his collection to his family and friends and presented the town of Accrington, Lancashire with the rest.

At the time his gift of unfashionable Art Nouveau glass cannot have seemed very acceptable. It belonged to another, more affluent age and was irrelevant to the problems of Accrington, where unemployment was increasing because of a slump in the cotton trade and there was much poverty in the Victorian slums of the town. It is strange to think of light, bright, colourful, sophisticated Tiffany glass finding a place among the "dark satanic mills" of Lancashire — but great good fortune that it did, thanks to the shrewd foresight of Joseph Briggs.

The collection of 120 pieces — 67 vases of high quality, 45 tiles and eight mosaics — was displayed in the town museum by the corporation of Accrington and later transferred to the Haworth Art Gallery, where it remained unknown to American collectors all through the years of Tiffany's obscurity.

When the curator of Haworth Art Gallery had the Tiffany collection valued for insurance in the 1950s, the total for the 120 pieces was £1,500: Favrile glass vases at £5-£10, fine examples of Tiffany tiles at £2-£3 and the glass mosaic exhibition piece of cockatoos at a mere £50.

There is little direct information about the association between Louis Tiffany and Joseph Briggs — the American millionaire and the lad from Accrington who went to America to seek his fortune. But in an obituary on Tiffany in 1933, he is well

RIGHT: **Magnolia Vase created for the World's Columbia Exposition of 1893. It was made at a time when America wanted decorative opulence and magnificence; it is now too richly ornate and elaborate for modern taste.**

ABOVE: **Iridescent Millefiore vase.** In developing the millefiori technique of the great Venetian glassmakers Tiffany came to take his place beside them.

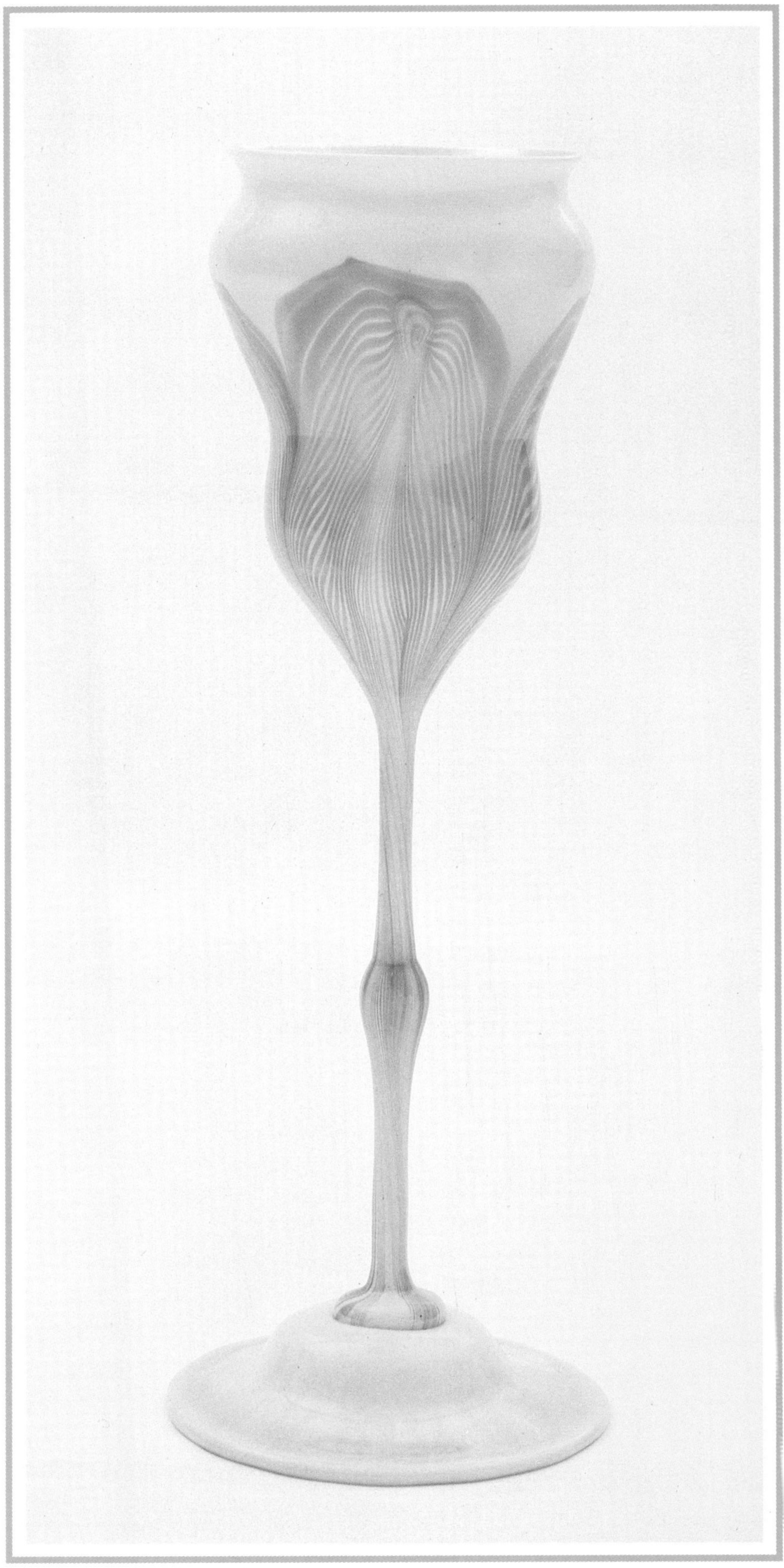

RIGHT: **It would be an insensitive eye that failed to respond to the artistry of Tiffany's slender flower form vases in Favrile glass.**

spoken of: "Joseph Briggs, who for forty-three years has worked side by side with Mr Tiffany and conscientiously reflected the Tiffany spirit". Tiffany evidently had high regard for Briggs. Tiffany's grandson William T. Lusk, who took over management of Tiffany & Co from Charles L. Tiffany II, wrote: "I gather that Louis had complete faith in Joseph Briggs and entrusted the management of his company to him after his death."

At Laurelton Hall the Tiffany Foundation struggled with ever-rising costs. In 1942 a marine research unit took over the house, and after the war the Louis C. Tiffany Foundation obtained permission to sell off the estate and fund art scholarships with the proceeds so that it could continue to encourage young American artists.

The entire contents of Laurelton Hall were sold at auction in New York in 1946. The treasures of a lifetime's collecting, from Mazarin blue rugs to Indian baskets, were sold at a fraction of their original value. A derisory amount was given for a signed piece of Favrile — $20.

A few years later the hall itself was sold with a four-acre plot for just $10,000. It had been valued 40 years before at $2 million.

To complete the extinction of Tiffany's glory, Laurelton Hall was destroyed by fire. Fire had been a recurring destroyer throughout his career, and always he had rebuilt and recovered. His reputation began to revive from the ashes of this fire 25 years after his death.

All through the 1930s and 1940s his name had been "cloaked with derision", as the Bauhaus functional and austere German style was adopted in America. Glass, it was thought then, should be transparent, ornament was anathema, a profusion of colour was vulgar. Tiffany was condemned on all counts: too ornamental, too colourful, altogether too richly decorative and at the same time too commercial. In a volume on American glass compiled in 1941, Tiffany was dismissed in a single reference under the heading "Fancy Glass".

But early in the 1950s an interest in Tiffany glass began to emerge among antique dealers and museum curators. Nikolaus Pevsner made reference to Tiffany and Favrile glass as an expression of Art Nouveau in his book *Pioneers of Modern Design*, published by the Museum of Modern Art. A few collectors — the painter Theodore Stamos and the art historian Milton W. Brown — began to acquire unusual examples of Favrile glass. In 1952 an Art Nouveau exhibition at the Kunstgewerbe Museum in Zurich gave Tiffany his rightful place on the scene and

for the first time the unique quality of his designs was acknowledged.

During the next decade interest in his work continued to grow. There was a revival of interest in iridescence: interior decorators began to take an interest in his ideas. In 1955 an exhibition of his work was held at the Morse Gallery, Winter Park, Florida, with a display of various Tiffany windows.

Stuart Poreston, art critic of *The New York Times,* wrote: "It will be an insensitive eye that fails to respond to the artistry of his hand-fabricated Favrile glass." In *Time* magazine, Tiffany's distinctive style was characterized: "In an age when man's vision seems increasingly hemmed in by a machine-made environment, there is an urge to draw new strength from adventuresome craftsmen who knew how to combine richness with beauty."

Gradually, Tiffany glass tiles and lamps and other items were being incorporated into interior designs: good examples of Favrile vases were on their way to becoming collectors' items, valued as period antiques, their style and quality characterizing the high point of American decorative arts in the Art Nouveau style; and art historians began to mark Tiffany's place as a gifted and original artist.

Another major step was taken in the re-establishment of Tiffany's reputation as a pioneer of modern design when the Byzantine chapel he designed for the World Fair of 1893 was resurrected in Winter Park, Florida. The Morse Gallery of Art, now at Winter Park, has the most important collection of Tiffany material in the world today, some 4,000 items. America had finally become aware of its outstanding indigenous designer and realized that he had been shamefully neglected.

Just a year after the fire destroyed his monumental mansion at Laurelton Hall, a retrospective exhibition of Tiffany's work was put on at the Museum of Contemporary Crafts, New York. Sarah Hanley, his last protégée, lent several items: his grandson Louis Tiffany Lusk lent a child's silver and copper dinner set designed for him by Tiffany. Ten pieces of jewellery were shown. Thomas S. Tibbs prepared a superb catalogue of his work, and in the process inspired a whole new generation of American collectors.

As the search for more examples of Tiffany glass began, collectors discovered the unique collection at Haworth and tried to buy it. Fortunately, the town of Accrington had developed its own pride in the treasures of Briggs's bequest and refused to sell.

RIGHT: **These millefiori vases of abstract design show Tiffany as an early exponent of pure form and colour in art expressed in glass.**

Robert Koch first came across the work of Louis Comfort Tiffany in 1956 when he was studying architecture at Yale University and preparing a paper on armory buildings in New York City. He found that Tiffany had decorated the Veterans' Room and Library for one of these.

Intrigued by Tiffany, his work and his place in art, he bought a Favrile glass bowl for $4, which he thought expensive. His wife disliked it and asked: "How long do we have to keep it?" In keeping it, they both came to enjoy it and see its value multiply.

Koch presented a paper on "The Stained Glass Decades" in 1957 in which Tiffany played the leading role, as was his due. The book he then began to research, *Louis C. Tiffany, Rebel in Glass,* involved meetings with Tiffany's grandchildren and led him to Laurelton Hall, only just before it was destroyed by fire.

When he began to write the book it was still difficult to locate Tiffany items, but interest in Tiffany was growing very rapidly and when the book was published, it sold out in two weeks. By the time it was reprinted, two years later in 1966, notable items were appearing: for example, the window designed by Frank Brangwyn and made by Tiffany for Samuel Bing's Art Nouveau exhibition at the Grafton Galleries

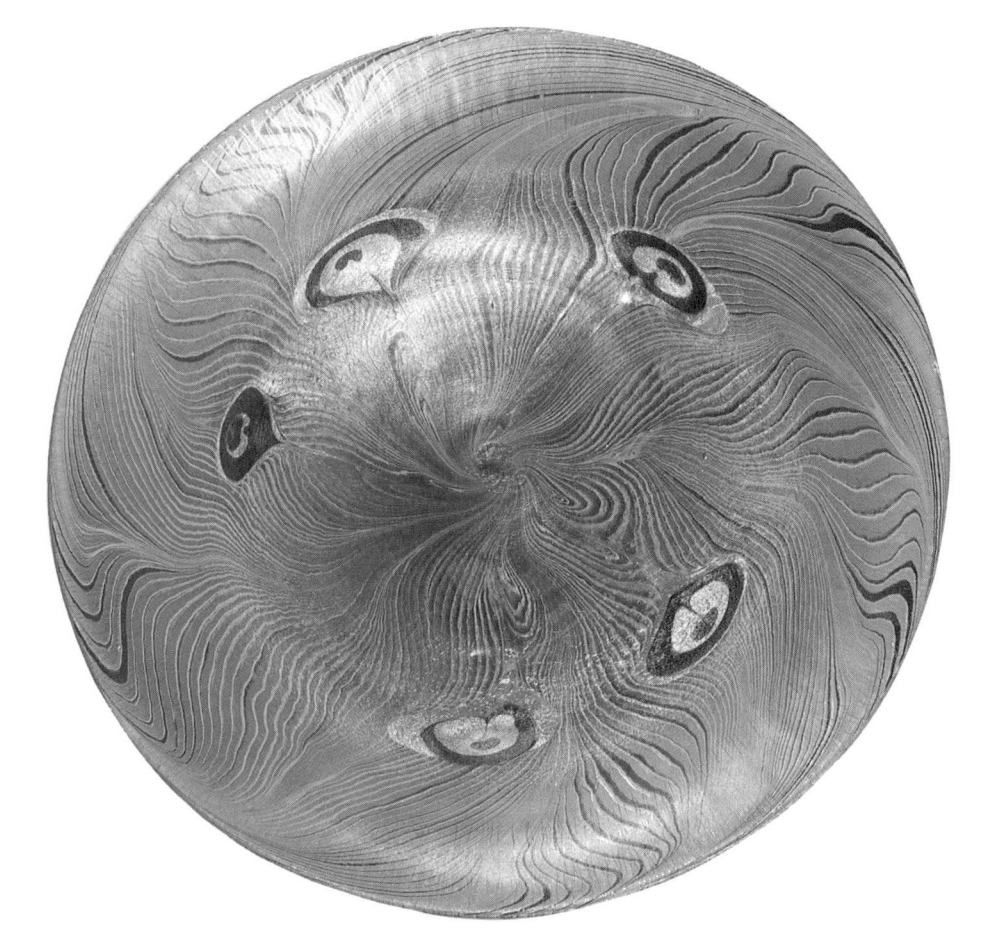

in London in 1899; an elaborate punch bowl made by Tiffany for exhibition in Paris in 1900. And Tiffany glass had more than doubled in value.

A third edition was produced 18 years later, by which time a whole new body of literature had appeared on Art Nouveau and the role of Tiffany: his lamps, his windows, his Favrile vases. But Robert Koch's book remains the definitive biography.

The publication of the book had considerable effect on Robert Koch and his family. They assembled a major collection of Tiffany glass; his wife became a dealer instead of a teacher, as she had intended; and they were among the first to exhibit Tiffany and Art Nouveau at antique shows. They were involved with the first of the many, many restaurants to install Tiffany lamps, and they worked with other collectors, discovering Tiffany items stored away forgotten in museum storerooms.

Together with the increase in interest and value came the appearance of forgeries, imitations and reproduction items that has made the task of the collector more complicated. It has become necessary to identify the genuine products with proved provenance, and work continues to classify Tiffany hallmarks. The name of Tiffany has become a generic term for any glass that is opalescent or iridescent, but not all of it is true Tiffany.

The rediscovery of Tiffany coincided with the reappraisal of Art Nouveau in the 1960s. Perhaps there was something about the rebellion against classical restraints expressed in Art Nouveau that appealed to the liberated 1960s. The curvilinear style, the free-flowing hair, the feminine gentleness and romance of much of the sensuous designs found an instinctive response at the time of the flower people. The love of the natural, with a hint of the bizarre and overtones of the erotic, appealed to a new generation that was throwing over harshness, austerity and restraint and was looking for beauty. And in so doing, was meeting with the same kind of hostility

LEFT: The technical
brilliance of this large
Favrile glass plate with its
swirling peacock design is
the essence of Art
Nouveau.

from the old order that the turn-of-the-century artists had faced from the Victorian establishment.

Interest in design came to the fore in the 1960s as the post-war generation began to find its style. People began to discover that the work of the Art Nouveau designers looked surprisingly modern.

The advent of Abstract Expressionism in America brought Tiffany to the attention of painters in this genre like Jackson Pollock and Robert Motherwell, who saw him as an early exponent of pure form and colour in art expressed in glass form.

Mario Amaya, writing in the book *Tiffany Glass*, published in 1967 wrote:

> In fact, Favrile glass appeared as an uncanny precedent to Abstract
> Expressionism; and when America's first great international
> contribution to contemporary painting was hardening into a
> movement in the early fifties, Tiffany glass which itself depended so
> much on the principles of controlled accident, color, shape, and free-
> form design — found new admirers.

It began to be realized that the unique quality of Tiffany that marked him out as an originator who could not be copied by those who followed, was the freedom with which the glass was handled. It was seen that, without violating the character of the material itself, Tiffany and his craftsmen had produced an amazing series of blown-glass objects decorated in the very highest order of good design. And Tiffany's skill in embodying accidental effects to enhance the glass and its decoration was seen as well ahead of its time.

Edgar Kaufman Jr wrote in an article in *Interiors* magazine: "Accident, the casual effect, was, furthermore, his approach to ornament, iridescence, acid etching, flowered or marblized patterns that swell, stretch and converge according to the craftsman's puff and twist at the glass."

Hugh McKean, who had studied at Laurelton Hall and became a major collector of Tiffany glass, commented: "Here are 'free forms' sometimes thought of as originating in The School of Paris. The clean line of modern art is here too. There are fresh shapes and colors and textures here, the creation of Mr Tiffany. In this art there is the daring and adventure of creation. These qualities keep art always new and always modern."

The increasing interest in Tiffany art glass was soon reflected in prices. They spiralled upwards dramatically. The Briggs bequest, for example, which had been valued at Haworth at £1,500 in 1957, is today estimated at £1 million. The cockatoo mosaic valued then at £50 today is £130,000.

Prices had risen even by the mid-sixties, as an article for the *International Antiques Yearbook* indicated: a set of four Favrile vases had sold for $70 the set in 1946. In 1966 the same four came up for sale again at the Parke-Bernet Galleries, and three of them sold for $2,500 each; the fourth, an ochre and blue iridescent vase in urn form with a wreath of leaves and vines, sold for $3,250. A dragonfly lamp that had cost $125 brand new in 1928 sold for $2,250 in 1967.

Dragonfly lamps, particularly the hanging head variety with an undulating rim to the lamp, are now highly sought after, and sell in excess of $80,000 in Christie's New York sales.

Christie's report that the trend is ever upwards for all Tiffany glass and the market is now well established. Because Americans like his work so much, the highest prices are in the New York sales and European collectors go to the Tiffany sales there. Lamps go higher in price than the vases today.

The highest prices are for the large wistaria lamps with the undulating rim — in excess of $120,000 — and the lily light clusters. In a December 1988 sale in New York an 18 lily light was sold for $46,000.

A Decorative Arts sale scheduled for 1989 includes a great variety of Tiffany lamps, familiar ones such as the apple blossom lamp and the Oriental poppy, at estimates ranging from $15,000 to $70,000; unfamiliar ones, such as the crocus pattern lamp, the pomegranate, the black-eyed Susan, the woodbine and swirling leaf patterns, together with various dragonfly shades, ranging from $60,000 to $90,000; a flower form vase of slender and elegant shape from the Lilian Nassau collection is estimated to fetch $60,000 to $80,000.

Sotheby's also report that sales of Tiffany are ever upwards in price, with both vases and lamps doing well. A miniature wistaria lamp from the Elton John collection sold recently for £33,000, a set of goblets for £2,100.

Bonham's report a steady rise in prices too. The market is strong because Tiffany is held in high regard in America and because his work is so very

RIGHT: The beauty of this piece of Favrile paperweight-glass vase is in the fluid sensual style of the decoration and the subtly glowing colour.

LEFT: **Jack-in-the-pulpit vase, the shape perfected by Tiffany to display his shimmering golden glass at its best.**

much of its period and period-looking. An example of a Tiffany daffodil table lamp in the sale of the John Robertson Collection of Art Nouveau and Art Déco in April 1989 sold for £11,500.

It is interesting in 1989 to read the *Financial Times* review of the art market dated November 1970. It cited then a Tiffany glass and bronze dragonfly lamp that had sold for £804 in 1967 and £2,917 only three years later; a gooseneck vase in the Persian style that had fetched just £11 in 1946 reached £155 in 1967 and £340 in 1970. The report states:

> The real market in Art Nouveau is less than ten years old. Specialist sales, which are now held regularly in Paris, London and New York, did not take place much before 1965 and the general level of prices before that date was so low as to have little or no relevance to the sums which have been paid during the past three or four years.
>
> It is no denigration of Art Nouveau to say that it is one small area of the art market which has been 'rediscovered' in recent years to meet the demands of an enormously increased body of collectors of works of art in general. After almost sixty years of neglect it was a rediscovery that was long overdue.
>
> At the beginning of the 1960s, Art Nouveau was the province of a small band of dedicated and — so they were then considered — eccentric collectors. Today the reverse is true — no style or type of art has such a wide appeal. Not only is this due to its highly decorative quality but also to the fact that it is still relatively inexpensive to form a representative collection.
>
> One of the most important subsections of Art Nouveau is Tiffany glass, produced by Louis Comfort Tiffany in America. This type of glass ... is greatly in demand among American collectors and for this reason — quite apart from its high quality — is one of the most expensive types of Art Nouveau.

There is no doubt that Tiffany would have thoroughly enjoyed the praise, the appreciation and the high prices for his work — and considered it the tribute due to his genius.

Looking back on his success 100 years later, it is clear to see how he stands out, overshadowing anything produced at that particular time by his sheer range and quality. The turn of the century was rich in fine glass. Gallé in France is usually classed now as the greatest of the glass-makers of the period, but Tiffany is more than just the most important American; he moved the technique of art glass into a different plane. Before his time lamps might have been designed with a decoration of wistaria; it was Tiffany who went further and created a lamp that is a tree — blossom, leaves, trunk, roots and all.

Tiffany clearly had a shrewd understanding of the value of publicity and was never loath to blow his own trumpet. He not only claimed the limelight when it was his due but seems, on several occasions, to have kept others out of it when it was more their due. But again, it is easy to see from this distance in time how the swings of fashion and fortune must have made it difficult for him to keep his balance. The time when he was the height of fashion — when to have a house actually decorated by Tiffany himself was the true mark of sophistication, when to have a Tiffany window was essential in every nouveau riche home from New England to the Middle West, from Seattle to San Francisco, when no home was decorated properly without a Tiffany lamp — was heady stuff for any artist. These were the artistic status symbols of their day, instant badges of culture.

On all sides he won praise and prizes — and often the praises went as much over the top as his own self-praise. Samuel Bing is often quoted because his words have the authentic *fin-de-siècle* sound to them. Bing's declaration that Tiffany's lustre glass, with its "opalised radiations, so subtle, delicate and mysterious that the water of an exquisite pearl can alone be compared to them", added to the force of the reaction against Tiffany when the time came. It was all too much — too sickly, too gaudy, rather vulgar.

The earnest efforts of Tiffany and other designers to make things of use beautiful, declaring that they were the "educators of the people in the truest sense", did not go down well with a younger generation with their own ideas and their own rebellion against the immediate past. They found it irksome to be lectured by Tiffany to the effect that they would do best to learn from *his* art, *his* design, *his* understanding of beauty.

RIGHT: A circular
enamelled copper wall
plaque with a decoration
of nasturtiums.

There remains today the opinion of some critics that Tiffany is more
kitsch than genius, a feeling that he went too far, did not know when to stop,
did not pay enough attention to the classical traditions. There are some art
critics and antique dealers for whom Tiffany art glass, and even more so, Tiffany lamps, will never be art or antiques in the true sense.

With his re-establishment, high claims have been made for Tiffany,
hailing him as avant-garde, ahead of his time, forerunner of abstract expressionist art; but at the same time, there has been continuing criticism,
condemning him as a commercial maker of vulgar "wedding present" wares.

Certainly, some of the Tiffany Studios production became repetitive, and
Tiffany's high ideals could not be maintained at the rate of output demanded
of him. But he was the first industrial artist, and the mixture of highly creative
artistic and technical skills with commercial production was a new and difficult role to control. In fact, it continues to make Tiffany difficult to classify.

Tiffany has been described as a man of immensely varied talents who fre-
quently talked and created meretricious rubbish. He declared his intention to
bring beauty to the masses, yet only the privileged and wealthy could afford
his work. He argued throughout his life that the decorative arts were more
important than fine art. He insisted that his stained-glass windows were a
pure expression of stained glass because all the colour was in the light and no
pigment was obscuring the light through the glass; yet with his use of opalescent glass it could be argued that he was obscuring the light just as much and
spoiling the translucency of the glass.

It is easy to see why Tiffany was attracted to the art of stained-glass windows: he loved colour, light, glass. He responded as an artist to the beauty of

the great gothic cathedral windows, and set himself to produce his own unique versions.

Yet his insistence, with his own success in America, that the best American stained glass, particularly his own, rivalled the greatest medieval windows, offended and infuriated many people. It was *"bizarre manifeste"*, as one French critic described it, and many English people have rejected his stained glass altogether pointing out that it was something quite different to medieval stained glass.

Tiffany was commissioned to design memorial windows on a commercial basis and succeeded in producing effective windows that pleased his customers. The windows of the Middle Ages, wrought by craftsmen of awesome faith and dedication, told the stories of the scriptures to those who could not read and showed the way to God. Some experts in stained glass feel that Tiffany did not fully understand the spirituality of the art, or that it was essentially a daylight art. A stained-glass window is seen from the light refracted through it; the colour changes according to the time of day, the season and the brilliance or dullness of the weather. Stained glass could be adapted to work with electrical lighting, as Tiffany did in *The Dream Garden* and the Mexican Theatre curtain, but this was a different craft.

Nevertheless, it remains true that there are many highly creative works, the result of Tiffany's zeal in experimenting, which achieve the synthesis between form and decoration that make them perfect examples of Art Nouveau — most particularly, the elegant attenuated flower form vases. He first became famous for his stained-glass windows and then for his lamps using the same techniques; his place as an artist is upheld by his Favrile vases at their best.

Tiffany had many imitators. Handel and Co, for example, produced a large range of decorative glassware, particularly lamps remarkably similar to Tiffany lamps. But they were copies; he was the originator. They might at their best rival him, but their general quality was of a standard he would never accept, including elements such as imitation leading on glass domes. The Quezal Glass and Decorating Company made products similar to Tiffany's glassware because it was started in 1901 by two of his former employees, registering the trade name Aurene for resplendent gold wares in 1904.

RIGHT: **The Peony Lamp — Tiffany's work is now highly sought after, the trend in prices ever upward and lamps go even higher in price today than vases.**

LEFT: **Favrile glass was well ahead of its time, fore-shadowing Abstract Impressionism with free form design and casual, accidental effects that could never be repeated.**

OPPOSITE: **Red is one of the most sought after Tiffany colours and is rare and costly today. The colour was derived from compounds of gold.**

In England, where glass production had been in decline since the high point of the 1880s, with their cut glass from Thomas Webb and Sons and fine cameo work by the Stourbridge glass workshops, most English glass was still very Victorian in character at the turn of the century, except for the glass design of Christopher Dresser at Whitefriars. His clean, sharp styles, long, slender shapes, applied trailed decoration, and use of streaks of colour, air bubbles, imperfections and gold inclusions as part of the decorative process were inspired by Tiffany. Dresser worked with Tiffany on many branches of design and shared the same Japanese influences. As well as basing his designs on plant forms, Dresser also appreciated the Ancient Roman and Middle Eastern glass that had so deeply influenced Tiffany at the start of his career.

Dresser and Tiffany can also be compared for their skill in handling the medium of glass. Both believed that the beauty of the material itself should never be spoiled, that shapes should enhance the sensuous quality of blown glass, not distort it.

Tiffany and Gallé had an originality and genius in the medium of glass that few could match. It became in their hands a medium of personal statement of ideals and vision, not just a vase or a bowl or a lamp. Their sheer artistic qualities mark them out within their own period. The international acclaim that was accorded to them was their due. Both have taken the test of time and their places in decorative art are no longer subject to the swings of fashion.

It is interesting to note that Tiffany always has a particular appeal to women. The most critical comment tends to come from men. Perhaps women delight in Tiffany's work because there is something essentially

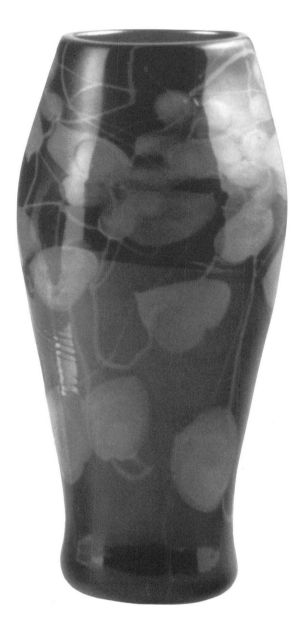

romantic about his creative imagination, his sensual feeling for form, his love of colour and for natural organic shapes, for flowers and beautiful insects. Tiffany's concept of beauty as an expression of a harmonious whole achieved through the unique properties of blown glass finds a more immediate response with women.

The Tiffany name remains synonymous with glamour and luxury, beauty and colour, iridescence and opalescence and richly glowing light.

It is very difficult today for anyone to discover any Tiffany glass hidden away in attics and storerooms, neglected in junk shops, going for a song. The hunt goes on, but collecting Tiffany glass is now a hobby for the rich.

Much of Tiffany's small glass is today in private collections. Much of his stained glass and mosaic in private and public buildings was destroyed or dismantled when it was considered too ostentatious for modern times.

A list of Tiffany stained-glass windows in America appears in Alastair Duncan's book, *Tiffany Windows*. It is described as "A Partial List of Tiffany Windows", extends to 20 pages of three columns and is still incomplete. It

gives some idea of the vast range of his work in this field, for the list does not include the domestic commissions, nor the religious and institutional windows undertaken after 1910.

The largest collection of Tiffany glass in Europe — now some 130 pieces — can be seen today at the Haworth Art Gallery, Accrington, Lancashire. Here some of the finest pieces ever produced are permanently displayed to fine effect. The extraordinary series of events whereby the gallery came to be the home of the Tiffany collection through Joseph Briggs's bequest adds to the fascination of the display.

The Haworth house is solidly Edwardian and reflects the prosperity of the Haworth family. It stands in a fine park of many acres. The principal suites of rooms, now forming the gallery, are panelled and carved with a Tudor theme. The gallery gives a unique opportunity to see Tiffany's work — the iridescent gold Jack in the Pulpit vase, the peacock feather vase, iridescent millefiori vases, cameo glass and lava glass. It is clear that the collection is treasured there. Curator Norman Potter, who supervized the setting up of the collection, is devoted to its subject.

At the Victoria and Albert Museum the collection of Tiffany glass is more difficult to locate. There is no catalogue for the display of glass in Room 131 and the information supplied on the showcase shelves is sparse.

But it is interesting to see the display of Tiffany glass in the same room as the Ancient Roman glass in soft colours, the Persian perfume sprinklers and the Syrian glass that inspired its creator. He takes his place with the Venetian goblets, the latticinio glass of the 16th and 17th centuries, the Bohemian glass painted in sepia enamel and the English cut glass by Ravenscroft

Two shelves of Tiffany glass — a collection of about 15 pieces, green, gold, brown, red, iridescent with trailed decoration — light up in the shafts of sunlight under the high domed roof of the Victoria and Albert. The colour glows with magical depth and brilliance. The last word on Tiffany must be that he was an outstanding colourist.

Tiffany himself puts it with characteristic grandeur: "God has given us our talents, not to copy the talents of others, but rather to use our brains and our imagination in order to obtain the revelation of True Beauty."

Cameo vases with a theme of lilies. Tiffany's place as an
artist is upheld by vases such as these.

# INDEX

# BIBLIOGRAPHY

AMAYA, Mario — *Tiffany Glass* — Walker & Co., New York 1976

CAPOTE, Truman — *Breakfast at Tiffany's* — Hamish Hamilton, London 1958

DUNCAN, Alistair — *Tiffany Windows* — Thames and Hudson, London 1980

GARNER, Philippe — *Glass 1900, Gallé, Tiffany, Lalique* — Thames and Hudson, London 1979

KLEIN and BISHOP — *Decorative Arts 1880-1980* — Phaidon, Oxford 1986

KOCH, Robert H. — *Louis C. Tiffany, Rebel in Glass* — Crown Publishers, Inc., New York Third edition 1982

LEE, SEDDON and STEPHENS — *Stained Glass* — Artists House, London 1982

LEVY, Mervyn — *Liberty Style, The Classic Years 1898-1910* — Weidenfeld & Nicholson, London 1986

NEUSTADT, Egon — *The Lamps of Tiffany* — Fairfield Press, New York 1970

PAUL, Tessa — *The Art of Louis Comfort Tiffany* — Apple Press Ltd, London 1987

POTTER and JACKSON — *Tiffany* — Octopus Publishing, London 1988

SPEENBURGH, Gertrude — *The Arts of the Tiffanys* — Lightner Publishing Corp, Illinois, 1956

All quotes from Louis Comfort Tiffany taken from his lectures and his book: *The Art work of Louis C. Tiffany* by Charles de Kay published by Doubleday, Page & Co., New York 1916 in a limited edition

# ACKNOWLEDGMENTS

The author would particularly like to thank Norman Potter, curator of the Haworth Art Gallery for his expert help, the staff at Sotheby's, Christie's and Bonhams for up-to-the-minute information on prices. Also my husband John Booth for editorial advice, Malcolm Nicolls for additional research on stained-glass windows and Celia Robertson for typing the book on disk.

## PICTURE CREDITS

KEY; t=top; b=bottom; l=left; r=right; f=far.

The author and publishers have made every effort to indentify the copyright owners of the pictures used in this publication; they apologize for any omissions and would like to thank the following:

American Red Cross: pp. 72, 73, 74, 75
Bonhams pp. 5
Bridgeman Art Library: pp, 33, 41, 63, 64, 65, 69
Bridgeman Art Library/Bethnal Green Museum: pp. 174
Bridgeman Art Library/Haworth Art Gallery: pp. back cover, 14, 15, 16, 17, 24, 78, 79, 95, 97, 98, 99, 101b, 103b, 106t, 113b, 126, 135, 143, 150, 151, 157, 163, 170l, 173, 181, 184, 185, 187
Bridgeman Art Library/Metropolitan Museum of Art, New York: pp. 169
The Brooklyn Museum, New York: pp. 43, 44
Christie's Colour Library: pp. front cover, 13, 20, 21, 36/37, 47, 67, 91, 93, 111, 116b, 130, 136, 137l, 178, 183
Corning Museum of Glass, Corning, New York: pp. 9, 68, 71, 101t, 105, 152
Frances Benjamin Johnston Collection — Library of Congress: 61b
Mark Twain Memorial, Hartford, Connecticut: pp. 58, 59, 60
New York Historical Society, New York City: pp. 11, 29, 50, 53, 57, 61t, 81, 153
Sotheby's Auctioneers, London: pp. 19, 23, 27, 49, 55, 102, 103t, 106b, 107, 108, 112, 113t, 115, 116t, 117, 120, 121, 122, 124, 125, 129, 133, 137r, 145, 146, 147, 149, 167, 170r, 177
Courtesy of Tiffany & Co: pp. 32